POWER
The Infinite Game

Michael F. Broom
Donald C. Klein

HRD PRESS, INC.
AMHERST, MASSACHUSETTS

First Edition

Copyright © 1995 by HRD Press, Inc.

ISBN 0-87425-269-2

Publication design by Page Design Services
Cover design by Art Torres
Editorial work by Mary George

CONTENTS

INTRODUCTION

We began work on the Energy Model of Power in the summer of 1977. Its current form is the culmination of 25 years of collaborative thinking and continuous invention. Our thinking has been molded by, and leavened thoroughly with, the thoughts of other writers in the field and, more importantly, the ideas offered by the several hundred participants in the Power Programs we conducted during those years, particularly at the NTL Institute for Applied Behavioral Science and at Johns Hopkins University. These participants helped us test, revise, retest, and revise again all of those collective thoughts.

The title of this book is also our slogan for the power model: *Power:The Infinite Game*. And power is a game, although in a particular sense of the word *game*. Many people regard a game as a pleasant but trivial pastime, a way to enjoy an evening with family and friends. Others find the word *game* suggestive of deception and manipulation, as in *con game*. Still others equate *game* with *competition*, whether that competition be friendly or ruthless. While these are viable meanings of the word, none accords well with our purpose here, for the subject of power demands a serious approach and sense of responsibility. We thus have taken a more generic view of *game*, defining a game as *any set of activities that has rules and participants and, sometimes, winners and losers.*

With this definition in mind, we will be exploring in the first chapter, and in the book as a whole, two fundamental and virtually opposing perspectives on power. One, the finite perspective, views power as a win/lose proposition. The other, the infinite perspective, holds the possibility of playing the game of power in a way that could be satisfying and productive for all. The book explores and contrasts these two perspectives by taking an in-depth look at how we generally play the power game finitely and how people might play it infinitely.

Chapters 2, 3, 4, and 5 deal with the day-to-day dynamics of power. Chapter 2 looks at power as the use of energy and the ways we convert that energy into intellectual, emotional, and physical effort. Chapters 3 and 4 explore the ways in which we attempt to connect our energy to that of others through influence—successfully or unsuccessfully. Chapter 5 explores the dynamics of how our influence with others is maintained at either high or low levels of satisfaction and equity, or is cast aside altogether.

Chapters 6 and 7 focus on the ways that we, through finite perspectives of power, disempower ourselves and attempt to damage others in defense of our sense of self-worth while attempting to avoid the humiliation that losing too often offers. Chapter 6 deals with personal issues of disempowerment, and Chapter 7 with social disempowerment or social oppression.

In Chapters 8, 9, 10, and 11, we describe how we might play the game of power infinitely and in an empowering way for satisfaction, joy, and productivity on behalf of ourselves and those with whom we live and work. Chapter 8 explores the basic actions of empowerment. Chapter 9 explores ways of discovering our Inherent Excellence, the bedrock upon which sits our notions of power and empowerment. Chapters 10 and 11 describe the concrete and specific activities that are the ways of empowering oneself (Chapter 10) and empowering others (Chapter 11).

We have been writing and rewriting this book for eight years now. We have survived our internal power struggles, our power struggles with each other, and the power struggles that just seem to show up in everyday life. We hope that we have benefited enough from those struggles to make this book as meaningful to you as writing and living it has been for us.

Enjoy!

CHAPTER ONE:

FINITE AND INFINITE PERSPECTIVES OF POWER

Have you ever...
Had so many things to do that you couldn't get them all done to your satisfaction?
Felt that job and family were more in charge of your life than you?
Been virtually paralyzed by fear of failing?
Been so angry that you could barely control yourself?
Felt worn out at the end of the day with not much accomplished?
Felt that no one ever pays much attention to your thoughts and ideas?
Wondered why some people seem to treat you so poorly?
Felt that life at work seemed to be just one power struggle after another?

Or, have you ever...
Worked on a difficult project with such intensity and focus that it turned out perfectly, just the way you knew it would?
Felt so strongly about something that nothing could have gotten in your way?
Been able to turn potential enemies into proactive partners?
Felt mildly guilty that your colleagues and family seemed to be giving you so much more than you were giving them?

What has your life been like? The first list of have-you-ever's? Or the second? If you're like most of us, your life has been and probably is now some mixture of the two; that is, some mixture of feeling powerless and feeling powerful. Most of us would like our lives to be like the second list—feeling and being satisfied, productive, and powerful with and in our lives. For those of us who would like to feel more power in our lives or for those of us who would simply like to be less abused by the power of others, increasing our own power and influence is a means to those ends.

Can you think of a situation in which power is not an issue, whether unresolved or resolved? Think about any of your personal, professional, or social relationships. Who is going to get his or her way this time? Or next time? You? The other person? Both? Suppose you have yielded several times to an associate's wishes and, therefore, feel you should get your way the next time a decision must be made. In such a situation, you would be dealing with an unresolved power issue, one that could turn into a power struggle.

However amicably power issues are resolved, they nevertheless remain power issues. For example, someone might think, Isn't it nice that my mother has finally stopped trying to get me to live my life her way? Despite the resolution, a balance of power still exists. Likewise, even in situations where we are so comfortable with the power dynamics that they seem nonexistent, the issue of power is at hand. A husband and wife may enjoy a wonderful evening at the ballet after looking forward to it for months, and the issue of power may be the farthest thing from their minds, but this does not mean power dynamics are not at work; it simply means these two people have their power focused in the same direction.

Let's establish our definition of power. First, consider the definition of power in physics: Power equals mass times velocity. Now consider the definition offered by the world of electronics: Power equals resistance times voltage. In either case, power is a force always moving and making something happen. Whether in the world of physics, electronics, or human dynamics, *power is energy in use.*

From such a perspective power is neither categorically good nor bad. It can be likened to a hammer. A hammer can be used constructively, to build a very fine house, or destructively, to damage someone's property. Power is energy in use and labeled good or bad only according to our choice. Power, of itself, has no such ability to choose. This is an important point.

Many participants enter our Power Programs with the idea firmly planted in their heads that power is something of which to be very wary. In a word, dangerous—dangerous in the sense of Lord Acton's famous homily: "Power corrupts, and absolute power corrupts absolutely." And in the minds of many, if having power is bad, to seek power is even worse. That would make us "power hungry." We know that the best thing to do with power hungry people is to stay out of their way or, better yet, get them before they get us!

How did power get such a bad reputation? To find out, let's do an exploration of two fundamental perspectives of power and how it operates in the world. We call these perspectives *finite* and *infinite*. (For these terms and some basic ideas that helped the authors contextualize their work, we want to acknowledge Dr. James P. Carse and his wonderfully insightful book, *Finite and Infinite Games,* 1986.) The following chart briefly describes these two perspectives, whose most important features are then discussed in depth.

FINITE AND INFINITE PERSPECTIVES OF POWER

The Finite Perspective	The Infinite Perspective
Fundamental Supposition: Power is scarce.	Fundamental Supposition: Power is abundant.
• A zero-sum, win/lose game.	• A positive-sum, win/win game.
• The purpose of playing a finite game is to establish a winner.	• The purpose of playing an infinite game is to continue the game and maintain it.
• The finite view easily evokes defense of self-esteem and identity. Deception and secrecy are strategies of choice.	• The infinite view evokes cooperation and openness while not allowing others to use them against us.
• This is a game to be played very seriously whenever the survival of our self-esteem or identity is at stake.	• This is a game to be played well, though playfully, because our self-esteem or identity is not at stake.
• Differences are used to define who is winner or loser, right or wrong, OK or not OK. Differences are threatening. Conformity is valued.	• Differences stimulate curiosity, learning, and creativity. Differences are valued.

Continued on next page

Continued from previous page

The Finite Perspective	**The Infinite Perspective**
• Time is used as a measure to define win/lose and becomes a major source of stress.	• Time is useful for creating opportunities for win/win.
• Making choices and being responsible are threatening because of the possibility we will make a wrong, hence losing, choice.	• Making choices and being responsible are the underpinnings of freedom, productivity, and satisfaction.
• The rules of the game are more important than the players. Being caught playing outside the rules leads to loss through censure, disqualification, or other penalties.	• The players are more important than the rules. Playing *with* the rules is important to assure the flexibility and creativity needed to create win/win results.
• The finite game supports little creativity as all play must be *within* the rules.	• The infinite game supports much creativity through allowing *playing with* and *outside* the rules.
• As players, we freely choose to play finitely although we often lose sight of there being an alternative.	• As players, we freely choose to play infinitely whenever we remember it as a possibility.
• The finite must *exclude* infinite games.	• The infinite game can and does *include* finite games.
• This is the paradigm of choice when survival is a moment-to-moment issue.	• This is the paradigm of choice when growth and learning are primary goals.

THE FINITE PERSPECTIVE

A zero-sum, win/lose game based on the supposition that power is scarce. In the finite perspective of power, there is only a limited amount of power available for everyone's use. In a zero-sum game, any gain must be accounted for by an equivalent loss—everything balances out to zero—hence, zero-sum. For someone to gain more power, someone else must give up an equivalent amount—hence, win/lose. If you and I were playing a finite game of power and I wanted more power, I would have to take it from you. Such an action would decrease your power, of course, but that would be OK with me and could even be why I want more power. You might consider it dangerous to decrease your power on my behalf, however, since that would allow me to take unfair advantage of you if I so desired. Rather than give up some of your power, you might decide that the safer course would be to decrease mine. You may also reason that if I am to lose power, it might as well accrue to you as to anyone else. So there we are, caught up in a game in which we are bound to struggle together—to attack and counterattack, quite often in the name of preemptive self-defense. Clearly, a finite, zero-sum, win/lose approach to power is bound to get a bad reputation.

There is a promotion available, and Larry wants it. However, Gina, his competition, sabotages an important project assigned to him. He is better qualified, but she gets the job. Larry is furious! He wants revenge for the obvious injustice, so he does his successful best to make life miserable for her at every opportunity.

This is not an unusual scenario. The cast and script may change, but the plot remains the same. Win/lose in the long run turns into lose/lose. In one way or another, both parties end up diminished, diminishing each other and diminishing the system in which both are employed.

We, the authors, have invested much time and ego in achieving our academic credentials—Ph.D.s—thus proving to the world and ourselves how smart we are, that we are winners. Someone calling us "stupid" would be "usin' fightin' words." In fighting back, however, we would be proving how stupid we really are. To acknowledge that I did something wrong allows me the opportunity to learn something valuable that I didn't know before. From fighting I can learn no more than how to fight better, if that.

The purpose of playing a finite game is to establish a winner. And, by necessity of the zero-sum characteristic, to establish a loser. The loser, in order to recoup, begins another finite game which will have its winner and loser. Power struggle begets power struggle. Have you been in many relationships that were a continual series of such struggles? Are you in any such relationships now?

The finite view easily evokes defense of self-esteem and identity. Deception and secrecy are strategies of choice. An easy step away from the concept of finite win/lose is the concept of right/wrong. Winners are right; losers are wrong. Winning is good; losing is bad. Winners are great; losers are . . . well, losers, pitiable and insufficient. Add that only half of us can win at any point in time, and it is easy to see how very difficult it is to avoid the issues of self-diminishment, low self-esteem, and poor self-image that go along with losing. It is these issues of self-worth that form the basis of our dreaded feelings of powerlessness and that generate defensive reactions.

In the realms of gender, ethnic, and so-called racial differences, an even higher cost is paid. In the area of gender differences, men are better—or so we used to be told and as many still believe. There is little need to wonder why men tend to see power as good and women usually see power as bad. Trickier are the issues of ethnic and "racial" differences. Noel Ignatiev, in *Utne Reader,* describes the black and white "races" as socio-political categories used to justify "white" privilege (Ignatiev, 1994). These categories are related to ethnicity but are essentially assigned designations that may have little to do with skin color. A dark-skinned person of Italian heritage person would traditionally be favored over a lighter-skinned African-American. Regardless of these complexities, the use of racial and ethnic differences to define who wins and who loses is not new news. Our corporations and society are still fighting the notion that people designated as male or white are better than those designated as female or people of color. The organizational and social costs of such thinking are very high. Imagine the additional productivity that would become available if women and people of color didn't have to use a sizeable portion of their energy to fight systemic discrimination and outright harassment. Imagine the costs of litigation and pretrial settlements that would be saved if all were equally accepted and valued. Imagine the savings to be gained if finitely based drug abuse, crime, homelessness, and hunger were not problems. In our discussions of the infinite perspective of power, we will explore the increases in organizational and social productivity that would be available if differences were appreciated for their intrinsic value. Such productivity is in addition to that gained by eliminating wasteful activities.

This is a game to be played very seriously. Because self-esteem is so involved in the finite game, people play that game very seriously. After all, the survival of our sense of self-worth and well-being is at stake. Finite games easily become struggles of desperation and leave little time or energy for creativity, joy, or intimacy. Winning the game is what is most important.

Differences are used to define who is winner or loser. In the finite view, *difference* is synonymous with *division*. A person's status as a winner or a loser depends on which side of a dividing line that person falls. Often society has already arbitrarily decided what side is the winning side. Easily observable differences have been ripe areas for this activity. All of us have been taught who will be the winner and who the loser in the following arenas:

1. Time and space differences
2. Ethnic backgrounds and religious preferences
3. Racial differences based on physical appearance and style
4. Gender differences based on physical appearance and style

As regards time and space, we've been taught that more wins over less, that fast wins over slow, that big wins over small, and that first place wins over second place or any other place. You personally might not think this way; however, many people do. For example, those in the sports world certainly do—more points wins over fewer points, faster times win over slower times, and first is always the best.

In the world of organizations, we complicate things a bit more. More still seems better than less, big better than small, and fast better than slow. But, are they really better? The capriciousness of our finite thinking comes into play with a bit of devilment. More what? A bigger what? These become important questions. No one would argue that striving to increase revenue and exceed the competition's market share are unworthy goals. At the same time, the overkill of monopolistic or near-monopolistic practices frequently has led to the demise (or at least substantial reorganization) of those organizations at the hands of the law, in the name of the greater good. Ma Bell, IBM, and Microsoft are cases in point. Even without the law, organizations that become too dominant in a free marketplace often wish for better competition to allow greater price increases. A local television station that dominates its market by a 2-to-1 ratio has a very hard time increasing its prices when the competition is already charging a third less. The culprit isn't thinking that more is better than less; the culprit is automatically and indiscriminately thinking that either is better than the other. The CEO that strives toward less market share will surely not last long!

Let's move on to more usual circumstances. Internal organizational turf battles and empire building commonly originate from the socialized idea that more is better than less. Having consulted with a host of organizations, we have seen too many that suffer from having indiscriminately emphasized greater quantity over greater quality. The struggles of the American auto industry over the past 20 years illustrate a case in which success at making more cars at the cost of quality resulted in a loss of market share. The syndrome of crisis management stems from employees believing that responding to perceived executive needs as quickly as possible wins over a more thoughtful response. In the rush to please those with higher authority (who win over lower authority), poor quality information is often detrimentally delivered. Often the energy used to quickly respond to the wishes of authority figures would be better directed toward supporting higher quality goods and services for consumers.

From the finite perspective, faster is generally seen as better than slower, as if everything were a race—fast cars, fast computers, fast runners. It is just as traditional to think that more wins out over less— more money, more toys, more whatever. Bigger is generally assigned the victory over smaller—even the cost of supporting "bigness" is not cost-effective. Right is better than wrong—at the cost of risk taking, creativity, and innovation. In all these space and time differences, if we were to simply reverse the current paradigm, little value would be gained. Should slow be better than fast, less be better than more, low be better than high, we would only have a different set of winners and losers.

Players must play *within* the rules. In our modern society, one of the rules of the finite game is to win while minimizing damage to the loser. Physical harm as a means of winning is no longer legal except in the extenuating circumstances of self-defense or war. If too much damage is done, too many players become unable or unwilling to play. If that happens, the productivity and very validity of the game comes into question. Accordingly, it is important to play within the rules of the game to protect its validity. To play outside the rules and get caught leads to reprimands, penalties, and, ultimately, disqualification. The rules also allow the all-important winners to be selected. Again, one must play within the rules, or the validity of winnership itself is threatened. Respect is withheld from winners who are suspected of cheating.

Philip was 12 years old, reasonably popular, and a star on his junior-league soccer team. It was the training season of what might become a championship year for his team. It was also time for the election of team captain. Philip had dreamed for years of being captain of a championship team. However, Carl was as likely to be elected as was Philip. Not the natural athlete that Philip was, Carl was an unassuming kid who had made quite a success of himself because he had worked hard at his game.

Philip couldn't stand the idea that the honor he felt he deserved so much might be awarded to the less talented Carl. During a practice session the day before the election, the two boys were playing against each other. Carl was dribbling the ball toward Philip's position. Philip engaged him, their feet tangled, and both went down. Philip landed on Carl's knee—some thought a little heavier than he needed to. Carl's scream signaled the damage that was to put him out for the rest of the season.

Philip was elected team captain, but the team never seemed to rally around him, and it finished a sad third place.

Who except for Philip will ever know whether Philip hurt Carl purposefully or accidentally? His teammates' perception of the incident, however, left enough doubt in their minds that, although they elected him, they wouldn't completely follow him. The possibility that he had broken a cardinal rule—don't hurt people, particularly not your own team members—was enough to ruin him as team captain.

The rules of the power game, finite or otherwise, are only occasionally formalized and written down. Most often they are informally promulgated through cultural, organizational, and group norms. They are learned from our role models—parents, bosses, mentors, coaches, teachers, peer group leaders, and the like. Sometimes we learn them through verbal warnings for small transgressions. Other times we will learn the hard way through disqualification or broken dreams—like Philip.

The finite game supports little creativity. The finite game is static and protective of itself. Its structure and rules are more important than its players. Players can improve within the game structure, but the game itself can be improved only through the enormous risk entailed in becoming a rule-changer or visionary leader.

Whereas playing within the rules provides a sense of individual and group security, there is also a major drawback. Creativity and originality too often put one too far outside the rules and, hence, are dangerous. Copernicus and Galileo broke the rule that said do not speak in any way that might contradict Church doctrine. By publicly disclosing their discoveries that the earth was neither the center of the universe nor the center of the solar system, they directly confronted the church doctrine of their respective times. Both were severely castigated for their originality and creativity. In the finite game of power, one must play within the rules.

We as players freely choose to play finitely. Most people in Western or Westernized cultures assume that the finite perspective of power accords with the facts of reality, that it is the only valid view of power and power games. However, it is valid only in the context of the reality that we have been trained to see. Once learned, that reality is seen as immutable, i.e., not amenable to change. Consequently, the idea that players freely choose to play finitely is, for many, very difficult to understand, let alone accept. How difficult depends on how deeply ingrained are our cultural lessons.

The finite must exclude infinite games. The mathematical accuracy of this statement is obvious. Just as obviously, limitless power cannot exist within limited power, and a positive-sum game cannot be played inside of a zero-sum game. Beyond it obviousness, the importance of this statement lies with its obverse—the infinite can and does include finite games. It is discussed in depth, a few pages from now, within the description of the infinite perspective of power.

This is the paradigm of choice when survival is a moment-to-moment issue. The finite perspective of power is the perspective of survival. It was absolutely essential to the survival of the human race when we still competed with the carnivores of past eras to see who would survive by eating whom. Obviously, we have won that competition to the point where many of the species which were dangerous to us then are now in danger of extinction.

Beyond our basic survival, the finite perspective has provided our society with other important advantages, as well as some extraordinary difficulties. The finite "competitive edge," which is very deeply ingrained in our culture, is responsible for much of our truly remarkable technology. That technology has supported uniquely high levels of comfort and income for the middle and upper classes. Pleasurable and labor-saving electronic devices are abundant. For many, that technology has also been life-saving.

That same competitiveness and technology has also taken our planet to the brink of both nuclear and ecological ruin. Pain, anger, guilt, and loss of self-esteem are endemic in a culture that insists that at least half of us must be losers at least half the time. Too many of us suffer so much from these ills that our economic well-being is hardly a joy.

Even at its best, the finite game of power consumes much energy. When playing finitely, a great deal of energy is used protecting self and self-esteem from the encroachment of others. In the combat that is the essence of finite power struggles, individuals use a great deal of energy repeatedly proving, in game after game, that they are right, that they are OK—often in the face of considerable self-doubt. One must guard against even the smallest slip lest it proves one's undoing. For those who are lucky, there are places of respite with family, spouse, and friends. For the unlucky, those places are also places of combat. The only retreat to safety is withdrawal into oneself with the help of alcohol or drugs—a lonely place at best.

Since we have chosen freely to play finitely, even though we may have long forgotten or never knew that we have such freedom, *we can choose not to play finitely.* If we choose not to play finitely, what other option is left? The other option is to play the game of power infinitely.

THE INFINITE PERSPECTIVE

A positive-sum, win/win game based on the supposition that power is abundant. In the infinite game of power, the amount of available energy is limitless and abundant. To balance wins and losses is no longer relevant. Even the very idea of winning and losing becomes no longer relevant if energy and power are limitless, i.e., infinite. Accordingly, the anxieties of win/lose competition are unnecessary, as win/win solutions are always available.

Seen from the finite belief system, notions of infinite power are fanciful, idealistic, romantic, nonsensical, and unrealistic. Although pleasant, infinite views of power are neither prevalent nor popular in our society. Nevertheless, let's explore the distinctions of infinite perspectives of power.

There is a promotion available, and Larry wants it. However, Gina, his competition, sabotages an important project assigned to him. He was better qualified, but she got the job. Larry was furious! He wanted revenge for the obvious injustice, so he did his successful best in making life miserable for her at every opportunity.

Remember that scene? Played finitely, it could end in futility for both. From the infinite, win/win perspective, the scene would develop as follows. Larry and Gina's mutual desire for the same promotion would be acknowledged. Knowing that they will be important to each other's success regardless of who gets the job, they mutually decide to support each other in producing the best work possible. One of them suffers a disappointment from the immediate loss of the promotion. From the overall success of their work together, however, both end up being successful in the long run.

But that's not the real world, you say! In reality, Gina would still have sabotaged Larry and gotten the promotion. How do you play win/win when the other party doesn't? Within an infinite perspective, the possibility of a win/win resolution of a difficult situation can be sustained and implemented as long as at least one of the parties involved is willing to attend to that possibility.

In the finite perspective, promotions and money are units of measuring who's winning and who's not, who's OK and who's not. From the infinite perspective, the promotion and money are still desirable and useful, but they are no longer connected to any definition of self as winner/loser or OK/not OK. Larry is OK, regardless, and has nothing to prove, not even to himself. Not getting the job is a single event in the play of the game and does not require the label "loss." Gina's sabotage reflects how seriously she is playing her finite game. That has nothing to do with who Larry is, and he has no need for retribution. In fact, since she now has a position of more authority than he, she is, if anything, more important to his desires than ever before. Let's replay the scenario from an infinite perspective.

After much soul-searching, Larry puts his desire for revenge into perspective and rehearses an approach to Gina that he hopes will convey an infinite perspective. Now fully prepared, Larry walks into her office. He lets her know that her sabotage was unnecessary and that they probably could have worked out a win/win resolution had she come to him beforehand. He then genuinely congratulates her for her promotion and asks her how he could be of help in learning her new position.

She responds as defensively as Larry expected, denying that she had done anything of the kind. As he had practiced, Larry says, "Well, let's forget about it; it's in the past now. What I want to know is how I can help you in your new job." "Why would you want to do that?" she asks. He responds with, "I can do my job better and have more fun with your help, and you can do your job better and have more fun with my help. That's all." After a pause, Gina says, "Let me think about it."

What do you think her response might be after she thinks about it? Actually, no matter how she responds—pro or con—if he takes it as just another fascinating play in a game that has no end and no winners or losers, Larry will maintain his infinite perspective. It is likely that, sooner or later, Gina will begin to play infinitely as well. After all, what would she have to lose?

The purpose of playing an infinite game is to continue the game and maintain it. In an infinite game, the goal is to assure that play is continued. With no end, there are no winners and losers, only the process of the game and its players. To maintain the game, it's best if all players stay healthy and benefit from their involvement. To have a player leave the game out of fear, anger, or pain is threatening to the game itself, for such events give rise to troublesome anxiety in the remaining players. Consider the residual anxiety in organizations after a downsizing has been completed. However, if a player (or employee) leaves willingly for another game (or job) of his or her choosing, the player leaves happy and, in most cases, is ritually celebrated with gifts and blessings. Such celebration gives positive support to everyone affected by the transition.

Partnerships of all kinds—marriages, friendships, professional relationships, organizational relationships—work best from the perspective that they will be long-lasting and fruitful for all. Professional sports leagues (such as the National Football League and the National Basketball Association) are, ironically, good examples of organizations that promote partnership. Although the product they sell to the public looks like a finite game, they spend a lot of time and energy on supporting financial and competitive parity through revenue sharing and draft procedures that allow the teams with the poorest records to have first choice at the best new players. Organizations that understand the need for healthy partnerships with their employees put a lot of energy into organization-development efforts that support effective conflict management, team-building activities, and programs like total quality management (TQM).

The infinite view evokes cooperation and openness without allowing them to be used against us. We have already noted that infinite games are best played in a supportive, encouraging environment. People become involved in their work and do their best when they feel that they have the support and cooperation of their colleagues and bosses. They also express their emotions best in families with such an environment. When the threat of losing is removed, openly expressing our caring and compassion is never dangerous or not in our best interest. Free of the fears and doubts generated by finite games, we can be assured that it is in our best interest to care for all players.

Even competitive games are best when played infinitely with friendly cooperation, support, encouragement, and compassion. Players encourage and support their competitors by acknowledging a good play, a practice not unusual even in professional sports. In the more everyday arena of competing against friends, the players might even give each other helpful hints. A tip on correcting a tennis serve that has consistently gone awry or on more accurately throwing a football improves the competition and increases the joy of playing the game. An employee who helps a colleague might lose the next promotion to that colleague but then receive that colleague's support when a subsequent promotion is given. The short-term game will end with someone being acknowledged the winner. Yet, the outcomes of games played infinitely are just moments in the larger game of the ongoing relationship in which everyone wins in the long run. Players playing infinitely do not attach negativity to losing.

A concomitant of cooperation is openness. Deception and information hoarding are antithetical to playing infinitely. They endanger the players and risk the game coming to an end. If I do not know your needs, fears, and desires I cannot help you except by accident or good guessing. Clarity and openness help us to support each other and are hallmarks of the infinite game.

Within an infinite context, being open is highly functional. Yet, such openness may seem dangerous to advocate, for many people, playing finitely, will not resist using the mistakes and vulnerabilities of others for their own advantage and, we fear, our disadvantage. This raises the question of what sense does it make to play infinitely when others in the game are playing finitely? If, in the name of self-defense, we give free reign to our fear of losing, we will revert back to playing finitely, often with a preemptive attack.

Rather than give in to our fears, we can maintain our infinite perspective and still not allow others to use our cooperativeness and openness against us. Robert Axelrod's book, *The Evolution of Cooperation* (1984), is very instructive about this. In a fascinating use of computer simulation which allows many iterations, Axelrod describes a strategy called Tit for Tat that plays infinitely and evokes cooperation while not allowing itself to be taken advantage of. The context of the simulation is a game called the Prisoner's Dilemma which, like many others, is used to help groups understand the dynamics and difficulties of cooperation. In the game, each of two players must choose and act upon a strategy of cooperation or strategy of exploitation without knowing what decision the other is going to make. In the game, exploitation always has a higher pay-off than cooperation. However, if both sides choose to exploit the result is worse than if both sides choose to cooperate (Axelrod, pp. 7 – 8).

Tit for Tat, the most successful Prisoner's Dilemma strategy, has five rules (Axelrod, pp. 109 – 123) that we have paraphrased below. They are:

1. Do well for yourself by your own definition, but not as compared to others.
2. Use cooperation as your basic mode of operation.
3. Reciprocate both cooperation and exploitation.
4. Return to cooperation, your basic mode of operation, immediately after reciprocating any exploitation.
5. Be clear with other players about what you are doing when you reciprocate their cooperation or exploitation.

Paraphrasing Axelrod (pp. 53 – 69) for our purposes, there are six provisos about playing infinitely that speak to its strength and effectiveness:

1. An infinite player will *never* be the first to exploit.
2. An infinite player will never succeed *beyond* another player.
3. An infinite player will only be effective if it reciprocates exploitation at its *first* occurrence.
4. An infinite player can thrive in a wide variety of hostile and cooperative environments.
5. An infinite player over several interactions will evoke cooperation in an exploitive player unless that player is totally non-responsive and can only exploit.
6. A small group of infinite players *cooperating with each other* will be effective against even large groups of exploitive players.

If we are willing to consistently play infinitely—cooperatively, openly, and in concert with others, not only will we succeed in the long run, but we will also support those who tend to exploit to begin to play infinitely as well. Patience, persistence, and passion are required, and they will be explored in Chapters 8, 9, and 10, which explore self-empowerment and the inherent excellence we need to manage our fears effectively.

This is a game to be played well, though playfully. To play infinitely, both players must be satisfied without equivocation. They must play fully and well, to capacity or beyond—stretching the limits of their abilities. And they must do so playfully, not as if their self-worth were at stake.

Many of us mistakenly believe an infinite perspective means that we should allow the other person to win even if we have mixed feelings about doing so. On one hand, we feel good about the other person winning; on the other hand, we still feel like a loser. Anytime you feel as if you've lost, you have been playing finitely. "You win/I lose" is just as finite as "I win/ You lose," regardless of who arranged the outcome. The socialization of women to accept losing on behalf of others often supports "You win/I lose" behavior.

Differences stimulate curiosity, learning, and creativity. Differences are valued. From the infinite perspective of maintaining the game, differences between the players are acknowledged and valued. Differences are the only source of learning that we have. Fifty Albert Einstein clones in a classroom could learn nothing from one other. Each already knows everything the others know. Companies with cultures that promote conformity of dress, speech, and attitude are most often companies with too much conformity of thought to allow much real innovation.

The learning organization, according to Peter Senge in his book *The Fifth Discipline* (1990), is the organization that will be successful and continue that success in a time of accelerating change. Books, articles, and workshops on effectively managing employee populations of greater and greater diversity are legion. What has not been acknowledged, however, is that diversity is necessary to create a learning organization. Insufficient diversity, resulting from an overemphasis on conformity, occasions learning insufficient to meet today's needs. Organizations that affirmatively hire and promote women and people of color yet insist these employees conform to cultural norms dilute, often into non-existence, the diversity they claim to value.

Synergy is likely to become the next buzz word in the world of organizational productivity. With synergy, the whole is greater than the sum of its parts. As organizations push for greater productivity with fewer and fewer employees, the search for synergy becomes a must if employees (many of whom are still enduring the stressful aftermath of downsizing) are not to burn out from too many 70-hour work weeks. Empowerment programs that support individual excellence together with team-building activities that develop group innovation and group problem-solving skills build synergy. Effective empowerment programs support individuals and encourage them to be themselves, i.e., different from others. Effective team building supports empowered individuals and helps them synergize their differences toward something greater than the sum of those individuals. Diversity is required for synergy. An overemphasis on conformity limits potential synergy. TQM programs that do not focus on the skills of synergy building will go the way of other potentially effective but poorly implemented "flavor-of-the-month" management programs.

When we play infinitely, the synergy-destroying evaluative concepts of win/lose and right/wrong, which diminish self-esteem, become non sequiturs and irrelevant. In their place, synergy-enhancing activities, fueled by curiosity about, interest in, and appreciation for differences, occur in support of learning and increased satisfaction and productivity.

Imagine a company that makes and sells tools and operates from the infinite perspective. In this company the big-picture design engineers appreciate and understand the time-consuming, often nitpicking detail orientation of the manufacturing types. Conversely, the manufacturing types value the often dreamy, pie-in-the-sky musings of the design engineers. Because of this mutual appreciation, the conflicts that arise are easy to manage. When the engineers ask for their designs to be manufactured in two days when two weeks are required, or when the manufacturing people inform the engineers that one of their designs is simply impractical from a manufacturing perspective, no one gets upset. Instead they value their differences. The designers know that the detail orientation of the manufacturing types is absolutely critical to quality workmanship and high sales. They value the practical-mindedness of the manufacturing types, for it helps them refine their designs and improve workability. The manufacturing people are quite aware that from the musings of the designers come the product designs that have kept the company state-of-the-art for years. They often go to the designers for ideas on how to improve their machine tools. Of course, they also get a laugh from poking fun at each other's strengths. From the infinite perspective, their discussions of conflicts are often emotional and passionate, but without rancor. They insist on continuing their arguments until both sides are fully satisfied. The anger and blaming that too often result from the self-esteem-threatening "I've-got-to-be-right" atmosphere of the finite perspective do not occur.

In this organization regular meetings are held between and within departments. During these meetings, which often break into smaller groups, solutions to problems are brainstormed, as are implications of, and ways to develop, new ideas. The recruitment section of the HR department is

under the standing order to find potential employees with interdiscipli-
nary backgrounds. People on a second career path are prized. Engineers
with backgrounds in psychology or marketers with undergraduate minors
in the humanities are examples of the diversity they seek along with the
more normal diversity of women and people of color.

In a world operating from the infinite perspective, gender and racial differences would be viewed not only as spicy additions to the essential sameness of humankind but also as integral factors in improving the human condition. The contributions that women and people of color would make if invited to participate *fully* with men and whites in the game of power would certainly be remarkable. Moreover, the mutual learning produced by this perceptual shift would act as a vital key unlocking the harmonic potential of technologies, organizations, societies, and perhaps the entire world. We would see how differences can form harmonic relationships and how conflict can move toward resolution; in this way, we would appreciate the beauty of diversity just as we might appreciate the beauty of music, its forms comprising tonal differences linked in concordant ways. However, as the infinite view is eminently practical, we would most appreciate the transformative power of creating harmony from differences—the real improvements that can result.

In recent years we have witnessed many significant changes in the world: political changes such as the fall of the Berlin Wall, economic changes such as the trade accords from the European Community Council, and attitudinal changes such as the growing success of environmentalism. Underlying most of them is the burgeoning recognition that it is time to get practical—to review the meaning of differences on a planet whose citizens can no longer ignore one another or the ecological systems that support them. Clearly, this is a world primed for the adoption of the infinite perspective of power and its appreciation of differences.

In the corporate world, as the planet's economy becomes increasingly integrated, Western businesses are seeking new ways to increase productivity—and consequently, long-standing differences between businesses are being seen in a new light. IBM, Apple, and Motorola may seem unlikely bedfellows in the development of low-cost, high-power, reduced instruction chips; yet, bedfellows they are. Bechtel, Pacific Gas and Electric, and Mitsubishi have formed partnerships to develop and manage clean-air, combined-cycle power generation plants. We must remember, however, that although the development of intra- and interorganizational synergy can be a critical response to the need for increased productivity, the finite perspective of power is inimical to synergy; thus, the infinite perspective is essential.

A commitment of cooperation is openness. Deception and information hoarding are antithetical to playing infinitely. They endanger the players and create a risk that the game will come to an end. If I do not know your needs, fears, and desires, I cannot help you other than by accident or good guessing. Clarity and openness help us support each other and are hallmarks of the infinite game.

Within an infinite context, being open to the point of vulnerability is highly functional. It supports and ensures win/win results. It also affords us the safest position possible. If I have nothing to hide and willingly share my mistakes, vulnerabilities, and humiliations, then what can hurt me? Actually, I give you the opportunity to help me and, if you choose, to gain a friend for life. The most harm you can do is ridicule me. But as a person living infinitely, I already know that I am ridiculous and will laugh at myself with you. Or, you may simply go away, leaving me no worse off, or maybe far better off, than I already am. When living infinitely we can receive as gifts whatever the world offers us.

Playing with the rules is important. The infinite power game permits players to play with the rules and to continue the game on behalf of everyone involved. It is therefore a dynamic activity, flexible enough to meet the growing challenge of play and the shifting needs and differences of the players, as well as wide-ranging enough to include a vast assortment of players, situations, and other real-world factors. In stark contrast, the finite game confines thought and action to a set of fairly immutable rules; usually, whatever lies beyond the rules must remain there, in a realm of impossibility. Should any player step over the line, into that realm, he or she is disqualified. Such inflexibility gives individuals and organizations little space in which to increase productivity and answer to changing and widely varying needs.

Consequently, it is of utmost importance to reconsider what kind of power game we are playing, and to choose a game in which playing with the rules is permitted and even valued.

Playing with the rules also evokes a sense of playfulness about the rules, particularly those that do not merit change. From the infinite perspective, the rules are meant to help, not hinder, and surely not meant to damage anyone. Playing with the rules is not to be confused with refusing to play by the rules. The following illustrates this point.

About 15 years ago Michael worked for a mega-sized federal bureaucracy. During his first nine months there, he wasn't given enough work to fill his time. Being the free spirit that he decidedly is, he would show up anywhere from 15 to 30 minutes late each day. Shirley, his boss, finally asked him to show up on time, regardless of how little work he had to do, since being on time was a rule.

After several discussions, Shirley acknowledged that Michael's routine tardiness did not look good for either of them. He simply didn't believe her (she was white and Michael, black), self-righteously refused to change, and continued to show up at his leisure. He gained a reputation as an intelligent but uncooperative person, in other words, a troublemaker. When Michael resigned four years later, in spite of his reputation for high-quality work, he was still at the same pay grade at which he had been hired.

Michael thought he was refusing to take those silly rules seriously, but actually, by refusing to honor a rule that really was not harming anyone (including himself), he was taking the rule quite seriously, and acting to his detriment. Had Michael some sense of the infinite perspective, he might have been able to see that the importance of his free spiritedness and racial identity (in contrast to Shirley's) was a matter distinct from the rule of punctuality. In linking his sense of identity to the enforcement of a neutral rule and refusing to observe the rule, he gave the system little choice but to deal him out of the promotion game. Had he taken the rule more playfully, as just a part of the game, rather than so personally and seriously, who knows how far up in government service he might have gone.

Infinite players use, design, and change rules to support the continuation of the game. Static rules can threaten play and have no place in an infinite game. It is this ability to play with the rules that makes the game truly infinite. Even the extreme challenges of physical exhaustion, the hostility of finite players, lack of material resources, and death itself can be accommodated through effective rule design and redesign (Carse, 1986, p. 10). More about this later.

The infinite game supports much creativity. Although it is certainly possible to be creative within a finite structure, the extent of that creativity will be limited by whatever boundaries the rules impose. Imagine you are an artist who is taking a finite approach to painting a canvas. First, your creativity is limited by the space available on the canvas. Second, your own rules about what you should or should not paint limit you. And, your beliefs about the talent you bring to your work limit you. Imagine approaching the same canvas from an infinite perspective. There is infinitely more opportunity *beyond* the limitations of the canvas, *beyond* the limitations of what you think you should or should not paint, and *beyond* the limitations of your beliefs about your creative potential.

How can we ever get beyond such limits? First, we need to become aware of the rules that bind us. Second, we must acknowledge the possibility of going beyond them. Third, we should explore what lies beyond the rules, moving forward with little or no idea of what will be discovered or created. Consider the nine-dot problem below. Draw four straight lines connecting all nine dots without lifting your pencil off the paper.

As we think about this problem or try different solutions, most of us confine our movements, remaining within the boundary we create using the eight outermost dots. Yet, the solution requires going beyond the rule that tells us to stay inside the square. (For readers who don't know the solution, it is provided on page 29.) Now that you are aware of your self-imposed boundary, you can consider the possibility that there are solutions other than the one offered.

Keeping the above in mind, see what infinite solutions you can devise for the individuals in the following scenario—Pete, Beverly, and Pete's potential client. Also recall that effective rule design and redesign can accommodate extreme challenges.

Pete was president and owner of a small engineering firm that, because of its debts, was just barely breaking even. Its business over the next couple of months would mean the difference between survival and failure, particularly as far as the banks were concerned. Pete thus had quite a problem on his hands.

Unfortunately, Pete was also dealing with a more personal problem. Beverly, his wife, had left him six months ago complaining of his lack of emotional expression, his lack of attention to her and their two children, his generally sexist behavior, and his propensity to dismiss her complaints with an affectionate hug and kiss. Feeling devastated without her, Pete had recently attended a workshop on finite and infinite power, and had decided he wanted a reconciliation. Playing as infinitely as he could, he approached Bev with the idea of going away together for a week to get to know each other again and rekindle their romance. Beverly agreed and they set a date.

The week before their departure a new potential client called. The client was in a jam, needed immediate attention, and was willing to pay top dollar for it. That top dollar amounted to a $75,000 contract, enough to put Pete over the top for good. If he asked for a postponement from Bev, she would be extremely angry and, in all likelihood, never want to speak to him again.

In devising infinite solutions, the first step is to ignore solutions of the either/or, win/lose variety. The second step is to analyze your own reactions, noting the limitations you automatically imposed on the scenario. For example, did you automatically see Pete as having to choose between Beverly and his client? Did you decide that he would have to lose his client to keep Beverly? Did you decide that he would have to lose Beverly to keep his client? Is it really true that a postponement would be unacceptable to either? By taking mental note of whatever your automatic assumptions, you will discover some of the rules by which you limit your creativity.

Beyond the limitations of such rules, beyond the finite realm of our assumptions, opinions, and beliefs lies the infinite realm of unknown possibility. From the perspective of the finite, we call that realm *impossibility*. From the perspective of the infinite, this realm is the ultimate space of creativity. It is in the space of unknown possibility that we are able to be creative about our lives from moment to moment, inventing whatever will work to live life as a win/win game. Given the strength of our finite socialization, living in the infinite space of unknown possibility is a challenge requiring us to put aside strongly held beliefs and ideas. But then, providing people with help in meeting that challenge is one of the purposes of this book.

We as players freely choose to play infinitely whenever we remember it as a possibility. All of us have had the experience of playing infinitely —probably many times. Think, first, of the satisfying relationships you currently have in your life. These relationships have their difficult moments, but such moments aren't important given their infinite context of shared satisfaction and productivity. We have these relationship in our personal lives or at work. Next think of the relationships that have had infinite times within them, even if they ended acrimoniously or simply through the vagaries of time.

Make a list of the relationships that you have and have had which you have experienced as being played from the infinite perspective. Going through such an exercise is important because doing so reminds us that we have played and can play the game of power infinitely. We often credit the other person or some external circumstance for such instances, while taking little credit for ourselves. Chapter 6, Disempowerment: How and Why We Play the Finite Game of Power, is very helpful to building our skill in playing infinitely as it explores the ways we must stop playing finitely with ourselves. Chapter 8, The Actions of Empowerment, specifically deals with how to build the high equity partnerships that are the key to playing infinitely.

The infinite can and generally does *include* the finite. Being without limits, infinite games of power easily can, and usually do, include finite games provided that those finite games serve the purpose of continuing the infinite game. Most marriages work better when the partners agree to be sexually faithful to each other. Most organizations work better when their finite rules regarding performance standards are enforced. Setting finite rules within the flexibility of an infinite context can be useful and supportive of players wanting to play well and maintain the marriage game or the organizational game, as the case may be.

Ed and Rita had been dating for a while. They loved each other, liked each other, and had compatible value systems. At some point they began to talk about marriage. Ed, in sincere but finite wisdom disguised as infinite, very rationally made his case for an open marriage, one free from the commitment to sexual exclusivity. Ed believed that if two people truly loved each other, they would have no need to place boundaries upon each other's behavior. He argued that occasional sexual behavior with others was irrelevant to the primary relationship. Rita, having had enough, walked out, thus ending the game.

Sometime later, while reflecting on the matter in the isolation and pain of his loneliness, Ed, with 20/20 hindsight vision, realized his error. The end of the relationship was not at all worth the intellectual purity of what he thought was an infinite ideal. Actually, his insistence upon his "intellectual purity" was simply the very finite game of being right. He realized too late that the infinite easily and comfortably can include finite agreements such as sexual exclusivity. His need to be right in a disagreement, however, had been more important to him than maintaining his relationship with Rita.

The irony is that Ed had always been faithful to Rita, and he had no intention to be otherwise in the future. Unfortunately, he was valuing the finite above the infinite. He stuck to his point and lost his relationship. That's not bad if it works for you and the other person involved. It didn't work for Ed. He now understands that insisting upon being right is, at best, secondary to maintaining relationships and, at worst, inimical to doing so. The finite cannot contain the infinite.

Ed is now willing to maintain a future relationship through building and adhering to a finite set of mutual and *dynamic* agreements. We stress dynamic here because, in the infinite perspective, finite rules are useful only if they are managed in a dynamic way, i.e., infinitely. The following illustrates a marriage managed in such a way.

Bill and Susan speak of being in their third marriage. In their first marriage, the agreement was for Susan to manage the home and have and raise babies. Bill was the authority on almost everything and Susan identified herself as Bill's wife. This worked for them for 12 years.

Eventually, Susan realized that the role of submissive wife was no longer working for her. They spent nine tough months in couples' therapy working out a new set of rules. Susan developed a career of her own, and Bill shared fully in the homemaking and child-raising tasks. This was their second marriage.

Their third occurred as the kids went to college or otherwise left home. A new set of rules was needed if Bill and Susan were to be successful in managing the new intimacy that confronts couples when the distractions of child raising come to an end. Susan and Bill decided that their third marriage would be based on romance and drew up a new set of rules. They agreed to create romantic meals together at least twice a week. They installed a hot tub to share at least twice a week. They acted like newlyweds and indeed saw themselves that way.

In this way Bill and Susan lived their relationship infinitely. They changed their finite rules whenever those rules became insufficient for, or inimical to, maintaining the satisfaction and productivity of the relationship.

Fred at age 33 had been a bank branch manager for five years and was ready to move up. While talking to Jennifer, his boss, about his desires he was told that if he could further reduce his branch's error rates, there might be an advancement for him. Error rates were not a new issue for Fred; for some time now, he had worked to improve them and, as a result, they were currently at an average level. But he knew that further improvements would be hindered by two 15-year-plus employees, Lucille and Otto. Despite Fred's talking, cajoling, and threatening their work continued to fall just short of acceptable. Yet, because they weren't bad employees—they were always punctual, pleasant, and hard-working— Fred could not find it in his heart to dismiss them.

Given his renewed desire for promotion, he talked with Janet in the Personnel office about what he should do. Both Janet and Fred had taken the Power Lab, and so she confronted Fred with the idea that he was playing a finite game called "I don't want to hurt anyone, so I must be playing infinitely." She explained to Fred that by not insisting that Lucille and Otto live up to their potential and meet his performance standards, he was disempowering everyone involved—both of them, himself, and his branch. "For everyone's good," she said, "fire them both. Your documentation is certainly more than strong enough."

Fred "slept on it" for several nights (which included a few nightmares), decided that Janet was on target, and dismissed Lucille and Otto. He explained to them that their performance wasn't working for anyone, including themselves. Otto complained that he was being unfair. Lucille swore that they would do better given another chance. Fred fired them anyway. It was the most difficult thing he had ever done.

Three months later he got a call from Lucille thanking him. She said that she had been burned out for years and needed to retire. Now she was enjoying herself and her grandchildren quite thoroughly. Otto, Fred heard through the grapevine, was still angry at him but making more money working for an insurance company.

The field of drug-abuse treatment uses the word *enabling* to describe attempting to help someone by covering up for them, thereby ultimately harming them. To sustain the infinite game, the covert finite game of taking care of people who would take care of themselves quite well if they had to, i.e., enabling people, must end. Playing the infinite game calls for supporting people to do their best. If the rule of not making life difficult for people isn't working for all the players, including yourself, change the rule. They will survive and probably benefit as well.

This is the paradigm of choice when growth and learning are primary goals. Currently, we are afforded the opportunity to learn how to be the best that we can be and how to build productive partnerships with those who are different from us. There is no natural necessity to play win/lose among ourselves. Yet, because the finite paradigm is so deeply ingrained within our nature, to live and grow from the infinite perspective will take conscious thought and effort. Fortunately, both are well within our reach.

A BRIEF EXERCISE

Take a moment to think about your relationships at work and at home. You probably have some relationships that you are playing infinitely and some finitely. Which are which? Think about playing the finite ones infinitely.

You may find it interesting to return to this exercise after you have concluded *Power: The Infinite Game*. The remaining chapters will deal more fully with how we play the game of power finitely and why we do so. More important, it will also focus on how we can play the game of power infinitely. In returning to this exercise, perhaps you will find that you have gained not only a new perspective on power but fresh insights into your personal and professional relationships.

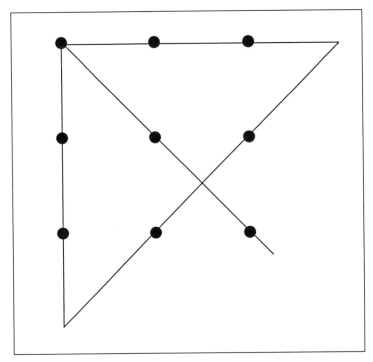

The solution to the nine-dot problem.

CHAPTER TWO:

POWER AND ENERGY

The discussion in Chapter 1 focused on defining power as energy in use and describing the features of the finite and infinite perspectives. We saw the power struggles that arise from finitely playing the game of power as well as positive results that derive from infinitely playing the power game. However, being able to fashion our behavior in accord with the infinite perspective requires an understanding of the basic power dynamics of human life.

THE ENERGY MODEL OF POWER

We are calling our description of these power dynamics the Energy Model of Power. It addresses the following four questions:

1. What is the energy of life that we use as power?

2. What are the ways in which we use and express our energy as power?

3. How does influence work so that others will cooperate with us or we will cooperate with others?

4. How can influence be maintained so that it is satisfying and productive for both parties?

Understanding the answer to these questions, then being able to apply that understanding, is key to becoming aware of the power that we all have and knowing how to effectively manage ourselves and influence others. The first and second questions are examined in this chapter; question three is discussed in Chapter 3, Influence Through Connecting, and Chapter 4,

The Seven Channels of Influence; and the fourth question is explored in Chapter 5, Power and Equity. Chapter 6 and 7 explore behaviors we would no longer use as we apply our new understanding, while Chapters 8 through 11 offer behavior changes to effectively apply our understanding of the human dynamics of power.

WHAT IS THE ENERGY OF LIFE THAT WE USE AS POWER?

If we are to use our energy more powerfully, it is helpful for us to understand the source of this energy that life puts at our disposal. Philosophers, mystics, and students of religion and spirituality have speculated about this question for centuries. They have all agreed on one basic idea: There is some type of universal life energy with which we are infused and from which each of us draws strength. Many different terms for this universal life energy are used — vital force and God are but two.

In the twentieth century, scientists began to discover and study smaller and smaller bits of physical material, the component parts of atoms. As they entered the realm of subatomic particles, they discovered that the physical world was not much like the world we experience through our senses. The world the physicists found does not comprise the solid arrangement of people and things; in their world solid objects do not exist—only energy exists.

In the view of modern physics, then, we really are not as physically solid as we suppose. We are, in fact, made of swirling fields of energy of different densities, very dense fields being called *particles*. Accordingly, it is quite appropriate to think of ourselves as energy beings. That is what we are as documented by the hard science of modern physics—swirling, radiating fields of energy of varying density.

Whether your speculations about the nature of human energy are metaphysical, spiritual, or scientific, there is some energetic *élan vital* which is the essence of human life. However ineffable this energy may be, an important insight is at hand—there is no such thing as *being* powerless. We might *feel* powerless; however, as long as we are alive we have the energy of life and can choose how to use it. Therefore, we can never *be* powerless.

Here is an exercise for you:

1. Think of a time when you felt powerless. This may take a moment.

2. Let that scene play through your mind from beginning to end as if it were a movie.

3. Identify what you were using your energy for even though you weren't getting what you wanted.

The key to this exercise is to identify what you were *doing* while you were feeling powerless. Many of us have found ourselves in situations with too much to do and not enough time in which to do it all. You have three projects that must be completed in two days, your mother-in-law is about to show up for a week-long visit, your secretary is on vacation, and your boss has just given you an emergency report to put together by the end of the day for his boss. This may not be the kind of situation where you feel powerless, although it would be for many of us. What we too often do in these situations is spend our energy blaming whomever we can identify as responsible for our predicament, complain about how unfair life is, worry about what awful thing will happen if we don't get everything done, berate ourselves for getting into such a pickle for the third time this year, or pick a fight with our spouse when s/he was just trying to help.

We call these non-constructive uses of energy *energy sponges*. We use these sponges to soak up tremendous amounts of energy without accomplishing very much. Clearly, there is no lack of energy or power considering the fine job that we do worrying, blaming, complaining, or arguing. We feel powerless, however, because we haven't been constructive. If we were to begin noticing when we have engaged in our favorite energy sponge, we then would have the opportunity to cease that behavior and attempt to find something more constructive to do, like asking for help or rescheduling. We might certainly *feel* powerless, but we can never *be* powerless.

To learn how to redirect the energy we put into our energy sponges, the next sections on the ways we convert our energy into power will be useful.

WHAT ARE THE WAYS WE USE AND EXPRESS OUR ENERGY AS POWER?

Energy Conversion and Uses

How does energy become usable to us? It must be converted—just as electricity is converted into light and heat to illuminate and warm our houses. As individuals, our first basic job is to convert our life energy into more specific forms that make it possible for us to work, solve problems, and play the many roles that we choose to play during our lifetimes. As writer and humorist Garrison Keillor might put it, we must convert our life energy into usable forms so that every day of our lives we will have the strength "to do what needs to be done."

As it is converted, energy takes three forms:
- Intellectual or mental energy
- Emotional energy
- Physical energy

Consider the following scenario in which the activity of going to the store figures prominently. Your mind, the storehouse of intellectual energy, recognizes that you are out of coffee and knows that you can buy more at the 7-Eleven. You have an important presentation to make this morning, which could lead to the promotion you've been after all year. You *really* want (emotional energy) to have your coffee, so you are willing to put out the effort even at six in the morning. You dress quickly, walk to the car, start the engine, shift into reverse, and so forth, using physical energy to carry out the motions necessary to get you to the store.

All of us convert our energy into intellectual, emotional, and physical forms. Yet, what makes some people more powerful than others and able to achieve their goals more often and faster? We don't know if some people are simply born with a greater capacity for energy and power than others, but we do know that the vast majority of people do not make the most of the energy they do have.

As we passed through life's early stages into adulthood, we all learned that there were certain ways of managing our energy that were OK and certain ways that were frowned upon or forbidden. These lessons helped us create behavioral patterns called *Power Patterns*. These patterns are mostly based in the finite perspective of what's right and what's wrong.

They tell us that if we use our energy in one way, we are right, but if we use it in another way we are wrong. With this in mind, let's take each of the three forms of converted energy and examine common Power Patterns for each.

Intellectual Energy

Intellectual energy is the energy that we use to absorb information, to make distinctions as a way of interpreting that information, and to make choices and set goals based upon those interpretations. This is the most prized form of converted energy in Western cultures.

This is an honor whose Western roots can be traced back to the rationalism of Plato through the Enlightenment of eighteenth century Europe, in which reason was the favorite word in learned circles. Among the philosophers produced by the latter period was René Descartes. For Descartes, we can discover truth that can lead us to further truths only after having methodically tested a principle beyond rational doubt. He concluded that only one principle stood up to such a test: *Cogito, ergo sum*—I think, therefore I am. This principle proves that we, in thinking, are conscious, intellectual entities. It does not speak to ourselves as physical entities; thereby creating a logical mind/body schism. In this duality, the mind is the only certainty, a finite victor over the body in our thinking about the source of truth.

This finite favoritism has fostered much of the low self-esteem and feelings of powerlessness that pervade our society. We might claim that smart people are clearly better than stupid people. What, however, makes one person smarter than another? And what exactly do we mean by "stupid"? Moreover, our lessons regarding quality and the use of our intellectual energy have a direct impact on how constructively we direct that energy and effectively develop our intellectual potential. Women were often taught that they were not, or should not be, smarter than men. Blacks were often taught the same with regard to whites. Others were taught that they were not very smart because they used their intellectual energy differently than their parents, teachers, or peers thought they should, as in the case below.

Ten-year-old Jan wasn't very interested in why things worked; all she wanted to know was how to make them work. Her mother was a teacher and her father an engineer. They bought her a computer, which she loved. At first, her parents were enormously pleased, but then a vague disappointment began to set in. Whenever they would try to explain to Jan how computers worked, she would sit politely through their explanations, then ask questions about how to draw a house using her graphics program. She rarely retained any of the data about how the programs worked. Her parents concluded that she just wasn't bright enough for the "whys" of computers. Jan noticed their disappointment and really tried to pay attention but not with much success. She just wasn't interested. Her personality preferred doing rather than conceptualizing, the opposite of her parents.

Jan was well into her middle twenties and moving up the ranks of construction engineering before she overcame her self-image as a not very bright person. Prior to that time she always deferred to "professional" people, who, as she had been taught, were always brighter then she. Having the benefit of hindsight she is now quite aware that she regularly kept silent about many of her fine ideas and acted upon the not so fine ideas of those professionals!

Being taught that she was not very bright, Jan rarely expressed her intellectual energy very effectively—not because she didn't have any, but because she learned not to value her energy in that form. Accordingly, she spent too many years seeing herself as personally insufficient. In fact, to keep a lid on the expression of her ideas, she actually had to use additional energy; consequently, that energy was *not* available for use toward her own goals. Given Jan's Power Pattern, she could not act with much power through her intellectual energy.

Another Power Pattern that can give us difficulty involves our taking on too many goals or conflicting goals. When we attempt to direct our energy in this way, we feel as if we are spinning our wheels and using up a great deal of energy while going nowhere. Most people have experienced the frustration of having taken on too many projects within too short a period of time. Some individuals, however, have a Power Pattern that tells them it's wrong to say no to anyone; and, therefore, they regularly have difficulty trying to do too many things at one time. Yet they, like the rest of us, are better off completing a few things well before proceeding to the remaining tasks. In this manner, we can focus greater amounts of our energy on each specific goal, thereby assuring a greater probability of success and sense of power. The idea that everything must be done at once is clearly a conceptual product of the finite perspective, in which time is used as a measure of who wins and who loses, rather than a product of the infinite perspective, in which time is seen as an opportunity to accomplish well whatever we choose.

More difficult and trickier conflicts involve tasks that are accompanied by some perceived risk. This point is made clear in the following scenario.

It is August and Craig is not happy with Barney, his boss. In March, Barney gave Craig an excellent annual performance appraisal and promised him a six-percent salary increase retroactive to the fifth of January, Craig's anniversary date with the firm. Craig has gently reminded Barney about his raise twice now, and both times he received apologies and assurance that it would be processed immediately. Craig realizes that he needs to take stronger action, since Barney has a history of getting caught up in his work and forgetting details such as other people's raises. On the other hand, Craig has never been comfortable being assertive with authority figures; such behavior never resulted in anything but grief the few times he attempted to be assertive with his rather autocratic father. There is also a possible promotion available within the next year, and Craig doesn't want to risk upsetting that apple cart either.

Finally, Craig gets up his courage to confront Barney after reviewing with his wife what he will say. With much trepidation he goes to Barney's office, and after much hesitation says, "Barney, you've got to process my raise now. I really need it!" Barney who has continued working, looks up in surprise. At which point Craig quickly says, "But if you're busy right now, I could wait a few more days. It's really not all that important." Barney's response is "OK," and he returns to his work.

On one hand, Craig really wanted to be assertive with his boss. The energy he could direct toward that goal was, however, very much watered down by the energy he was putting into the opposing goal of wanting to avoid upsetting Barney. He associated his boss with his father, but Barney and Craig's father actually had little in common other than their stature as authority figures. Again, a split focus splits our energy, reducing our effective power, often to near zero. This stands in stark contrast to a clear and singular focus that allows us to be engaged fully in getting what we want.

A final Power Pattern that saps our intellectual energy and distracts us from achieving effective power in the world is one that directs our efforts toward protecting and maintaining our sense of identity.

David stuttered through his formative years. He was also asthmatic, which contributed to his always being the second smallest kid in his classes. Looking back on those years, David rather disparagingly referred to himself as having been a "social nerd." He saw himself as essentially unappealing to the opposite sex. He did, however, see himself as having one saving grace: He was smart.

In later years, though having outwardly overcome his shyness with women, he became somewhat depressed over his seemingly infinite state of unattachment. Whenever he found himself intimately involved with a woman, he would become defensive about the smallest things, display his intellect rather than share his love, and gear into full retreat from his paramour. At last hearing, David was still a single man.

While growing up, David taught himself—with help from others—that he was unappealing to the opposite sex and that his strongest attribute was his smartness. From his perspective, that was who he was, an unattractive but smart person; that was how he identified himself. Whenever the unappealing part of his identity was stirred by a woman genuinely attracted to him, he would throw up a barrier of intellectual acuity. He would automatically put his best foot forward—his smartness—to hide and make up for what he identified as his unappealingness. Such a strategy is clearly inimical to intimacy, and David had always been "smart" enough to get out of relationships that were not working. David's strategy with women also provided him with repeated proof that his view of himself was perfectly correct.

Over and above all else, we tend to focus our energies in ways that prove to ourselves the accuracy of our self-definitions. We feel powerful as we accomplish goals that are consonant with our self-definitions, and feel powerless in the face of goals that, if achieved, would contradict our self-definitions. As long as we see our self-definitions as serious and important *rules* about ourselves, rather than as simply *our stories* about ourselves, we will find ourselves falling into this power trap.

The more we apply the infinite perspective to ourselves by playing with our rules about ourselves, the more we will free our energy from the traps of self-definition. As we experience more and more freedom from the intellectualized *shoulds*, *musts*, and *have tos* of our self-definitions, we allow ourselves more intimacy with and acceptance of the fullness of ourselves, more intimacy with and acceptance of others, and more intimacy with the wholeness of the universe in general—a set of experiences that some call spiritual.

Spend some time noticing what your Power Pattern for intellectual energy is and whether it helps or hinders you. What were you taught about the value of intellectual energy? More important, what were you taught about the value of *your* intellect? Do you value your intellect more than you value your other energies? Less than you value them? How do you compare your intellect with others? How much energy do you spend trying to go in two or more directions at the same time? How much energy do you use protecting who you are? How much do you use defending or shoring up your self-esteem?

Emotional Energy

The recognition and the use of emotional energy are highly problematic in our society. We are taught that emotions are irrational and not to be trusted, that by necessity they stand in warring opposition to the intellect. Given the high value our society places on the intellectual, emotional energy is therefore denigrated.

This belief is not only very debilitating but also very odd. Emotional energy is the energy that fuels our sensibility; it allows us to care enough to put ourselves into action. If we don't care about a problem, for example, we don't do anything about it. To the extent that we *do* care and feel strongly about it, we use our energy to work toward a solution. Our emotions thus signal the need to act and reinforce the importance of action. Since power is energy in *use*, our degree of power is commensurate with the degree to which we use energy; therefore, emotional energy, which stimulates the use of all forms of energy, is of utmost significance. Rather than dismissing or reviling emotional energy, we should recognize how it is essential to the effective use of power.

The word *emotion* literally means "to move out." Its etymology can be traced through Old French to the Latin word *exmovēre, ex* meaning "out" and *movēre* meaning "to move." Thus, in a sense, to be emotional is the very essence of power. Of course, when emotion runs wild, lacking intellectual direction, it certainly can be problematic and potentially destructive. At the same time, clear intellectual consideration and direction without emotion get us nowhere. And in a culture like ours, which so values going somewhere and getting things done, isn't it paradoxical and more than interesting that emotions have been so denigrated?

The typical Power Pattern that wants to deny the value of emotional energy is debilitating for two reasons. First, we too often diminish ourselves when we are experiencing powerful emotions such as fear, anger, guilt, sadness, and pain. We cut them off as inimical to clear thinking. Actually, we can think just fine in the presence of emotions unless we have been taught that emotions get in the way of clear thinking.

Second, our self-diminishment grows worse as the restraint of our emotional energy and power decreases the levels of energy we need to accomplish our goals. Cutting off the expression of emotional energy requires an enormous amount of physical energy. To attain such control we tighten the muscles in our temples, our jaws, our necks, our backs, our stomachs, and so forth. This muscle tension restricts blood flow. By increasing muscle tension and restricting blood flow, we give ourselves aching heads, necks, backs, jaws, and may tax our immune systems as well. Without the power of emotional expression, we find ourselves feeling achy, tense, and tired as well as feeling impotent and frustrated.

Thomas is an engineer. He designs and builds bridges. He is very intelligent, as were his parents, both of whom were also engineers. His parents, like theirs before them, were not very demonstrative and taught Thomas the value of thinking clearly and working hard. He remembers to this day his parents telling him, "With a good brain you can accomplish anything you want, but never let your emotions get the best of you." Thomas would hear this whenever he had gotten into a fight (he didn't get into many), whenever he was frightened, or whenever he had hurt himself.

Now Thomas is in trouble. He feels dead-ended in his work. His boss gives him only minor projects. He has begun to wonder if engineering is really the right field for him. But, if not engineering, what? He'd like to talk to his wife about how he's feeling, but they've never had such conversations before, and he's not sure he should. To make matters worse, Thomas has not been feeling well. His stomach is constantly upset, he gets headaches fairly frequently, and he doesn't sleep well any more. He thinks about seeing his doctor but believes that if he can just think this thing through, he will know what to do.

Like too many of us, Thomas suffers from bottled-up emotions. He feels sick, stuck, and listless, and he doesn't know what to do about it except think some more. But thinking will not get him out of his trap. He has his emotional energy locked up in his body. He can't do his work well because he has never really cared about engineering. He can't get help because that would be a sign of being too emotional.

One of the paradoxes of the workplace is that, in practice, organizations emphasize attaining high levels of success—a province of emotion—while current organizational mythology holds that emotions should be left outside the workplace door. In truth, emotions are very welcome in the workplace as long as those emotions are constructively focused on getting work done. The emotions that are problematic stem from the frustrations of having too many priorities, too many deadlines closing in, too many projects, and too many interpersonal difficulties, such as uncooperative colleagues, personality conflicts, and unsupportive bosses. If we use emotion to vent, argue, ambush, complain, blame, diminish ourselves, and make excuses, we will find ourselves becoming unpopular with the powers-that-be and experience the attendant loss of needed influence. What then to do?

An alternative to letting those energy sponges soak up our inner resources would be to focus that same emotional energy on rebuilding relationships, negotiating for help, setting clearer priorities, and pursuing other problem-solving activities. However, before we can engage ourselves we must be willing to discipline our emotional reactions to serve the purposes of our intellectually made choices. Each emotion has its own goal. The goal of anger (in its lesser and greater forms) is to punish others for some perceived wrong done to us. The goal of fear is getting away from some perceived threat. The goal of excitement is celebration. Self-punishment is the goal of guilt. Left without the correcting influence of our intellect, our emotions would serve goals not useful to our organizations and too often not useful to ourselves.

As already stated, without emotion there is no movement, no motivation. And focused emotion is passion, without which our achievements are small, at best. It is time for us to honor emotional energy that is focused by intellectual energy. To take a personal step forward in this direction, spend some time noticing what your Power Pattern for emotional energy is and whether it helps or hinders you. What were you taught about the value of emotional energy? What are your beliefs about emotions? Which are OK? Which are not OK? How easily can you express how you feel?

Physical Energy

This is the energy needed for physical motion. All of the internal functions of our bodies use this energy. The beating of our hearts and our breathing are but two examples. Communication through acts of talking, walking, writing, gesturing, smiling, and frowning all require physical energy. Walking, running, jumping, and the like are more obvious activities requiring physical energy.

Purposeful physical activity (aside from reflexive activities like the beating of our hearts, breathing, and startle responses) is activated by the motivating force of emotion. Emotions that are out of control will activate physical activity that is out of control. Most physical actions are considered fine if they are not done with "too much" energy. Using "too much" physical energy is considered directly related to being "too" emotional. As in the case of intellectual and emotional energy, we have developed a set of beliefs about the appropriate and inappropriate uses of physical energy. Walking is almost always OK. Running is only OK in certain situations or for certain purposes, such as to get exercise. Running down the street or through the halls of your organization with your business attire on is not OK. Mild gesturing with your hands is OK. Broad gestures often are not. Hitting someone is definitely not OK. Speaking softly is fine, but shouting is frowned upon.

When we feel strongly enough about something and are about to embark on some physical action we believe would be inappropriate, we use additional physical energy (such as tensing our muscles or withdrawing) to restrain that action. On the other hand, when our intellectual energy is not conflicted and used to focus emotional energy into passion, we will put ourselves into very powerful physical action. Such action, when compared to our more normal modes of action, is characterized by dramatically increased productivity with a much higher probability of success. Such is the power that many of us seek.

What Power Pattern guides the use of your physical energy? Is it similar to your pattern for emotional energy? Do you express yourself as fully and as loudly as you would like to? Do you touch and are you touched as often or as strongly as you would like?

Moving Beyond Our Power Patterns

Clearly, a key to experiencing the power and effectiveness that is available to us lies in letting go of the constraints dictated by our Power Patterns. First, we must become aware of these largely unconscious patterns and realize the detrimental effects they can have on our lives. Among the possible effects are the following:

- Using our intellectual energy to focus upon multiple or conflicting goals rather than to concentrate on a single goal at a time

- Using our intellectual energy to verify our self-definitions rather than to point ourselves toward other goals that may benefit us more

- Using our emotional energy to contain our emotions rather than to experience and express how deeply we care about our goals

- Using physical energy to restrain our actions rather than to move strongly toward our goals

Second, from such awareness we can consciously choose how we will use these conversions of our life's energy to experience our full power on behalf of our personal satisfaction and overall productivity.

In the next two chapters we turn our attention to the second phase of the Energy Model: learning how we can use our personal energy to influence others to use their energy on behalf of our goals. Chapter 3 focuses on how we can connect our energy to that of others, and Chapter 4 includes an in-depth discussion of the energy channels through which such connection is possible.

CHAPTER THREE:

INFLUENCE THROUGH CONNECTING

HOW DOES INFLUENCE WORK SO THAT OTHERS WILL COOPERATE WITH US AND WE WILL COOPERATE WITH OTHERS

To be as powerful and effective as we would like to be, it is essential for us to have sufficient energy available. This availability depends on our knowing what we want to accomplish, on our caring enough to want to act, and on our having the physical capacity to do so. These are qualities that the individual player brings to the Game of Power. By themselves, however, they are very often not enough.

Life is rarely a solo act. We can rarely play the game as if we were playing solitaire. Think about it. We require the efforts and energies of other players to reach our goals and achieve our ambitions. We live in a communal society, regardless of the ethic of individuality for which our society is famous. We can succeed in our jobs only with the cooperation of our peers, subordinates, superiors, customers, or suppliers. We cannot even feed ourselves without the cooperation of our paymasters, supermarket personnel, and those who made or sold us our pots, pans, dishes, and other utensils. We can be happy alone, but only for short periods of time. We can manage our eliminatory functions alone, but that's about all. Only in cooperative groups have we humans succeeded in becoming the dominant race upon the planet. Again, think about it.

Because we can accomplish little through the use of our energies alone, we must find methods to get other people to work with us, cooperate with us, and otherwise help us get what we want. In this and the following chapter, we will discuss such methods, focusing on the second of the three basic questions that underlie the Energy Model of Power.

HOW CAN I CONNECT MY ENERGY TO THAT OF OTHERS SO AS TO GET THE COOPERATION I NEED TO ATTAIN MY DESIRES?

This question presents us with the challenge of finding *energy connections* between ourselves and others. These connections provide us with ways to link our energy with the energy of others in any particular situation. To develop a successful, hence influential, energy connection with someone, we must intentionally or accidentally tap into *their* beliefs about how they can be influenced. However right a possible way to connect seems to us, the connection won't work if the other refuses to accept it, does not notice it, or does not hold it as important. Be aware, too, that the other players in the Game of Power will usually be doing their best to influence you even as you do your best to influence them.

Imagine there is a connecting channel that runs from yourself to the other players. Through that channel flows influence. This influence is the use—on your behalf—of the intellectual, emotional, and physical energy of other players—their ideas, attitudes, and values; their motivations, ambitions, needs, and drives; their body movements and speech. Your degree of influence depends on the strength of the connection. If the connection is weak because there is lack of contact or because you and the other players mistrust one another, the channel will be narrow or blocked. Your influence, then, will be reduced or cut off altogether. If there's a strong connection, the channel will be open to a full and free flow of your combined energies.

The strength of the connection depends on how well the players relate to one another and on the issues involved. A connection that's based on trust, on agreement about goals and how to work together, on frequent contacts, and on a history of successful cooperation provides a solid base for influence. One marred by mistrust, serious disagreements, or infrequent contact does not.

In any situation it is important to do whatever one can to free the connecting channel of distracting clutter—the humiliating debris from previous embarrassments, static created by misinterpreted motives and missed expectations, and the tensions aroused by suspicion and mistrust. Obviously, a channel that uses frequent and open face-to-face discussions is more likely to encourage a fuller degree of influence than one that is limited to infrequent contacts and the use of formal memos.

Many connections permit the flow of ideas, information, feelings, and actions in one direction only, limiting energy flow in the reverse direction. Boss/subordinate relationships often feature this type of one-way influence, as do many parent/child and male/female relationships. The energy of the subordinate, child, or wife will conform to the direction set by the boss, parent, or husband, but not vice versa. Obviously, such relationships are being played from a finite perspective of power. According to what we have been taught traditionally, boss/subordinate, parent/child, and male/ female differences constitute a hierarchy in which the former *should* influence the latter, and not vice versa. Actually, almost any set of differences can be used and has been used to establish uneven, finite channels of influence. White/black, rich/poor, upper class/lower class are but a few other examples.

In finite power games the players seek to increase their influence and, at the same time, attempt to keep others from doing so. Finite power games are always win/lose in nature; that is, if one side gets what it wants, the other side fails to get what it wants. At one extreme is open conflict: If one side wins, the other must lose. The connection is adversarial, based on mutual distrust, fear, and the desire to overcome or destroy the opposition. The players circle each other like Japanese sumo wrestlers, each seeking to exert the leverage that will overpower the other. At another extreme, both parties tacitly, often unconsciously, have agreed on who is dominant and who is submissive, usually along the lines of traditionally socialized differences mentioned above.

In most cases, however, the players have worked out some balance of give-and-take. Both sides have an overriding interest in playing the game in such a way that the basic relationship offers some level of safety and comfort. For example, two workers who are competing for promotion at the same time will give-and-take with one another, if only grudgingly, in order to remain secure in their present jobs. A husband and wife may battle one another regularly over a certain issue, such as money or sex, but not carry their battles too far for fear of losing the security of the relationship altogether. In both examples the win/lose ethic still pervades; sometimes one gives in, sometimes the other.

In infinite power games the players, at some level, understand that their success depends on the success of those around them. Winning at the expense of another is a short-term win at best and an eventual loss in the long run (thus the win/win nature of infinite power games). The infinite connection is synergetic: the result of two or more players playing infinitely will be greater than the sum of the results of two players playing by themselves. It is based on understanding, trust, and the recognition that all people are worthwhile and necessary, regardless of differences in position, background, belief, or opinion.

Because players of the infinite power game embrace their similarities and differences, they are able to acknowledge differences in expertise, authority, and responsibility without using them to impose arbitrary limits on who can influence whom and on how influence must move between people. Carse expresses the essence of what influencing is like between players of the infinite power game:

"I am not strong because I can force others to do what I wish as a result of my play with them, but because I can allow them to do what they wish in the course of my play with them." (p. 31)

In a finite power game, Carse says, "Power refers to the freedom persons have *within* limits . . ." Whereas in an infinite power game, it refers to "the freedom persons have *with* limits" (p. 31). (Emphasis added.)

Beliefs About the Sources of Power

We now turn to ways in which influential energy connections occur. Let's begin with a hypothetical situation. Suppose that you're the owner-manager of a fast-food franchise in a highly competitive area. You decide that the only way to beat the competition is to ensure that your staff gives super cheerful, friendly, and speedy service. Think about how you would go about doing that.

Would you order your workers to provide better service? Fire a few of them as an example to others? Give frequent pep talks? Offer bonuses for outstanding service? Organize regular staff parties and outings? Tell them how much you admire and appreciate the work they do? Provide customers with a way to tell you when they've received especially good service?

Put the name of the employee of the month on a plaque? Send letters of commendation to outstanding workers, their families, and, for those who are students, their school officials? Hold regular meetings in which the workers themselves decide how to upgrade customer service? These are only some possible approaches one might take, all of which have been used with some success in the service industry. Did you come up with other approaches?

Whether we notice it or not, when we try to deal with the challenge of getting others to cooperate with us, we're guided by certain deeply ingrained ideas regarding ways we *should* attempt to influence and ways we *should not*. These ideas, which are the sum of our lessons regarding influencing and being influenced, come from three main sources: (1) what people in our society are generally taught, (2) what we have learned from subcultural lessons, and (3) whatever we have learned from our personal experience regarding what works and doesn't work in the world of influencing.

In a complicated society such as ours, conflicting ideas often co-exist in our minds. Anyone raised in the United States, for example, might believe that bosses are supposed to tell employees what to do, that "you can catch more flies with honey than with vinegar," that "nice guys finish last," that there are times when it's necessary to "kick ass," that you should "do unto others as you would have them do unto you," and that you should "love thy neighbor as thyself."

Our lessons also may omit certain possibilities that might have come to mind had we been raised at another time and in another society. For example, if you were the owner-manager of the fast-food outlet, you would be unusual if you threw a temper tantrum to get the workers to do what you want. Though the idea of throwing yourself on the floor to kick and scream might appeal to you, you would probably consider it inappropriate to do so. Neither would you be likely to call a prayer meeting with your workers to ask God's help to make them better workers; arrange for a witch doctor to perform an on-site ritual ceremony to cast out the demons of sloth, indifference, and discourtesy; arrange for staff aerobics at the opening of each business day; engage your staff in a ceremony using a psychedelic drug to invoke the spirits of joy and devotion; or schedule regular group meditation sessions.

The lessons/beliefs of our culture do not support such practices; therefore, such practices would not occur to most of us, and if they did, we would dismiss them as impractical, odd, even crazy. Other cultures with lessons different from ours might support such practices, if, of course, they had fast-food chains. If the culture of our industrious and dedicated owner-managers had taught them any of the above measures, they would be considered as appropriate and practical.

Seven Possible Options

Generally, there are seven kinds of channels through which we can influence others either to connect their energies with ours or to allow us to connect our energy with theirs. These seven channels are available to us whether we're playing a finite or infinite power game. These options involve the use of the following:

1. Position and Role
2. Coercion
3. Ability to reward people
4. Expertise
5. Attraction
6. Group solidarity
7. Networking with people

We can use any or all of these options in any given situation. In practice, however, we too often act as if our options are quite limited; that is, each of us favors certain options and rejects others. Some options seem more practical or ethical than others, and certain ones appear more in keeping with who we are or would like to be. Perhaps we're more skilled in using certain ones and unsure about how to use others, and as a result, rely on the former and reject the latter. Sometimes, we're not even aware that one or more of these options exist. Moreover, we're generally not even aware of the options we are using, nor of the possibility of using others. In any case, we unnecessarily limit our choices.

Power Patterns

Why do we so limit ourselves? The answer lies in the years during which we were taught, by experience or by human intervention, patterns of strategies by which we could connect our energies with others to influence them either positively or negatively to cooperate with us. For instance, like everyone else in the world, you began early in life to develop your own unique patterns—your Power Patterns. Even as an infant, you discovered that in order to secure what you needed, you had to find ways to connect with your mother. Later, the circle widened to include more individuals and a larger set of ways to get what you wanted and needed. Though these ways probably were far from perfect, they worked well enough to make it possible for you to survive and to get to this point in your life.

Because your Power Patterns were determined by the ways that, early in life, either worked for you, were rewarded, or at least seemed safe, these patterns are deeply ingrained and automatic; they have become part and parcel of how you define yourself and the kind of person you strive to become. Such is the case with each one of us. This ingrained nature makes it difficult for us to see how our Power Patterns can misdirect our energy and restrict the choices we make when establishing connecting channels of influence. And to the extent that these choices are restricted, our ability to use our available energy is limited.

The ingrained and automatic nature of our patterns also dictates how we let ourselves be influenced by others even when we don't want to be. This point is very important as it is a major source of our sense of powerlessness and the anger and depression that we experience when we feel trapped and victimized. For many of us, as has already been noted, our Power Patterns say that we *must* obey our parents, bosses, and other authority figures. The sense of *must* too often carries over into our adult lives, when we are no longer dependent on these authority figures for our sustenance and can easily manage any threats of punishment we encounter. Time and again we find ourselves feeling angry, trapped, and victimized when all we need to do is say no and act accordingly—so deeply are our patterns ingrained and obeyed. Since these feelings seem beyond our control, we get angry with those who appear to be taking advantage of us, or we turn our anger inward and berate ourselves for having been *so stupid* again.

As you read about each of the seven channels of influence in the following chapter, try to take note of your own Power Patterns. Notice your reactions to each channel. How do you feel about using it? How would you feel if someone were attempting to use that channel to influence you? Good? Bad? Indifferent? In what situations? How well does each channel fit your beliefs about how people *should* or *should not* attempt to influence others? The greater your awareness about your Power Patterns, the more possibilities you will have to transcend them and experience the power that is inherently yours. More about that in later chapters.

CHAPTER FOUR:

THE SEVEN CHANNELS OF INFLUENCE

In this chapter, our discussion continues to address the third question underlying the Energy Model of Power: *How does influence work so that others will cooperate with us and we will cooperate with others?* As we focus on the seven channels of influence, through which such connection is possible, please pause to consider how you might apply each channel to yourself and your situation in life. In doing so, keep your mind open to five thoughts we consider to be truths:

1. The more ways through which you can connect with others and influence others, the greater the possibility of your being influential.

2. Each of the seven energy channels is available to you. Depending on the circumstances, each of them can work.

3. You may choose, in practice as well as theory, to use any and all of the seven channels of influence.

4. There is no absolute rule that says that your own Power Pattern is any more or less honorable or ethical than any other.

5. To the extent that you know your Power Pattern, you will be influenced *only* when you consciously agree to be influenced and not feel victimized.

As a way to begin the presentation of the seven energy channels and of how people tend to limit their choices to certain ones, we offer the following case study.

Jessica Benson was the loan officer of a small local bank in Maryland's prideful Eastern Shore. She had grown up in a white, liberal, middle-class family with high expectations. A practical, no-nonsense person, she didn't spend time on vain regrets. Today, however, was an exception. She'd just turned down a business loan application from a former elementary school chum, Tom Chapple.

A member of an African-American family that had been living in the county from Civil War days, Tom was assistant manager and short-order cook in a local restaurant. He was a deeply religious person and devoted much of his spare time to youth work and teaching adult Sunday school at the large and well-attended Northside Tabernacle. In fact, he was an elder in the church and a member of its Board of Deacons. With his long-standing reputation for hard work, integrity, and caring in the community, he counted as fishing and hunting buddies the state senator from his district, a powerful member of the county council, and the governor's legislative aide.

After 20 years of working for others in truck stops and diners, Tom had saved enough money to make a down payment on a small diner in a rapidly expanding business district of the city. He applied to Jessica's bank to finance the mortgage.

The business idea itself was a good one. The problem was that in Jessica's opinion, Tom lacked three ingredients she believed were necessary to make such a business succeed: financial know-how, drive, and the ability to get other people to follow orders and be accountable. She therefore had turned down his loan application.

Though disappointed, Tom had not been crushed by Jessica's decision. "If it's the Lord's will for me to run my diner, He'll provide the way," he'd said as he left Jessica's office.

"I feel terrible," Jessica told her husband Richard that evening. "I've known Tom since we were children. He's a hard-working, decent man who deserves a break, and I wasn't able to help him. It's hell to have this kind of power over a person's life. Maybe I should have given him the loan."

Richard, a construction engineer who prided himself on being objective, wasn't convinced. "Not at all," he said. "Either Tom has what it takes to run a business or he doesn't. It wouldn't make sense to give him a loan when you know he'd probably fail. What kind of break would that be? Anyway, you were just doing the job the bank pays you to do. You can't let sentiment enter into your decisions any more than I can approve a bad bridge design just because I like the engineer who designed it."

To fully understand the power dynamics of this case study, let's first recall the seven channels of influence:

• Position and Role
• Coercion
• Ability to reward people
• Expertise
• Attraction
• Group solidarity
• Networking with people

At first glance, the dynamics of the power game here seem quite simple. They appear to involve only the channel of position and role: the relationship between Jessica's position and role as loan officer and Tom's position and role as applicant, which gives her final say over his request. Both Tom and Jessica agreed—prompted by the typical Power Patterns for this type of situation—that she had the right to grant or refuse his request. She refused and there it ended.

But did this power game necessarily have to end that way? Are the dynamics quite as simple as they seem? Let's look at other ways this power game could have been played given the other details in the case.

Coercion. Raised in a deeply religious family in rural Maryland during pre-civil rights days, Tom learned to succeed through a combination of hard work, a well-deserved reputation for reliability, and his religiously grounded love for his fellow human beings. His Power Patterns were based on these qualities. When an outraged Northside Church member proposed that Tom could easily have organized his many friends to take up his cause with Jessica and other bank officials, and even threaten a church boycott of the bank if necessary, Tom refused to consider the idea.

Remaining true to his Power Patterns—that is, to his self-image and self-ideal—was more important to Tom than getting the money he wanted.

Reward. Again, given his background, Tom did not have a barter mentality when it came to people in positions of responsibility. He believed that such persons should simply be allowed to do their jobs as they saw fit. Accordingly, it never occurred to him to suggest to Jessica that, as an elder in the large Northside Church and a member of its Board of Deacons, he could possibly send a good deal of business her bank's way.

Knowledge and skill. Because of her middle-class background, Jessica respected job expertise; however, it was automatic for Jessica not to recognize expertise in workers outside white-collar professions, such as restaurant people. As he would have been pitting himself against the strength of her pattern in this area, it may have done Tom little good had he emphasized his considerable amount of expertise in the restaurant business basing his argument on the many years he'd worked as a manager and short-order cook in a number of informal but successful restaurants.

Attraction. When a friend urged Tom to present an appeal to Jessica based on their childhood bond, Tom was very uncomfortable. Actually, their childhood friendship and his reputation as an honest, hard-working man were powerful factors in Jessica's mind, even though her husband dismissed them as irrelevant sentimentality. What might have happened, do you suppose, if Tom had chosen to make more active, deliberate use of the channels of friendship and reputation in his dealings with Jessica? Who can say whether Jessica would have decided to grant the loan?

Group solidarity. Tom and Jessica were members of the same small, proud, close-knit community. Tom could have called upon their shared sense of community membership as an additional reason for the loan to be granted. Such an expression of group solidarity might well have helped turned the situation around. Tom's emphasis on his strength as an individual would not allow him to do so.

Networking. Tom had a network of politically savvy friends who might well have been willing to support his cause. He was a fishing and hunting buddy of the state senator from his district, a powerful member of the county council, and the governor's legislative aide. Still, Tom's own personal pride would never have allowed him to do that.

Either Tom did not recognize the fact that he had additional ways to connect with Jessica, or he deliberately decided not to use them. We have seen that although Tom had access to six of the seven channels of influence, his Power Patterns did not allow him to use those channels in his encounter with Jessica. His patterns were grounded in deeply held personal beliefs that, in this situation, were strongly against the use of coercion, group solidarity, and networking, and simply did not include the possibilities of reward, expertise, and attraction.

Tom had a lot more going for him than either he or Jessica realized. They were too focused on the agreement that Jessica's position as loan officer gave him the right to apply for the loan and her the right to refuse it. Had Tom moved beyond the limits of that focus, pursuing the six other channels (any of which, singly or in combination, could have swayed Jessica's already ambivalent decision in his favor), she may have seen that Tom had enormous potential power and influence. The chances are that she and her bank would have considered Tom an excellent financial risk.

It is quite possible that Jessica may have made an unwise business decision. Given Tom's reputation in the community, his knowledge of the business, his influence within his church, the loyalty of his many friends and well-wishers, and his network of politically influential buddies, he probably would have run a successful diner. The irony is that his and Jessica's failure to factor in all seven of the energy connections contributed to the disappointment both of them felt when she turned down the loan. Keep this case study in mind as you read the following detailed discussion of the seven channels for connecting energy. We will focus on each channel separately. At the end of each section, examine your beliefs to see if they would allow you to use that particular channel depending on the situation and notwithstanding your ideas of right and wrong.

THE SEVEN CHANNELS OF INFLUENCE

Position and Role

There are people who would agree that position and role are equivalent to power. In this view, position and role confer on a person the right to direct the energy of everyone accountable to that position and role and, if applicable (as in the case study above), to accept or reject any services or goods overseen by that position and role. Social scientists have termed this type of influence *legitimate power*. We, however, do not see position and role as power but only as one of the seven channels of influence through which our power can be expressed.

What makes it "legitimate" for certain individuals to influence others based on such assorted factors as age, work responsibility, rank, and position in life? For the most part, law and custom do. Both law and custom in our society mandate that mothers and fathers assume responsibility for the well-being of their preadult children. Friends, neighbors, and relatives can be expected to express disapproval if a couple leaves small children unsupervised for long periods of time. Parents also can be held accountable by law for such behavior as child neglect and child abuse and, in some cases, for such things as damages caused by their unsupervised children's misbehavior.

Position and role as one of the channels of influence also involves rank, responsibility, and rights. To understand this channel better, let's take a look at each of these three features.

Rank. In our society, many of us have long taken it for granted that those of higher rank have the right to tell subordinates what to do. In fact, we use the phrase "to work for someone" as a way to emphasize that one person is working under the supervision and direction of another. The responsibility for organizational success or failure usually ends up with top management. Though managers may blame their subordinates when things go wrong, in the final analysis the buck stops at the office of the highest senior executive.

Rank is not restricted to organizations. We find it everywhere in our society. Parents outrank children. Police officers working in the line of duty outrank citizen bystanders. Physicians outrank nurses. The once-standard marital vow for women, "to love, honor, and obey," clearly meant that husbands outranked wives.

Responsibility. Responsibility is the obligation to direct one's energy toward the satisfactory performance of the duties connected to one's position. All positions have corresponding responsibilities, regardless of the nature or status of the position. Physicians have the responsibility to do their best to heal the sick, as teachers do to educate children, and as police officials do to enforce the law and protect public safety.

Rights. One's position—be it prestigious or low on the social scale—also involves certain rights, chief among which is the right to lay claim to others' energies in order to get one's job done. For example, in cases of emergency, a surgeon has the right to lay claim to the resources of a hospital's operating facilities, regardless of operating room schedules and routines established for usual surgical cases. A sanitation worker has the right to refuse to collect garbage that householders have not placed in sealed containers. Both are operating on the basis of position and role.

Position and Role in Organizations

You probably work in an organization. If so, your degree of influence in that organization depends, at least in part, on your rank and your responsibility. Where you sit in the chain of command determines those to whom you are accountable and those who are accountable to you. Very likely, there is also a division of labor, which means that in order to get your job done you're dependent on others from different parts of the organization, just as others are dependent on the specialized functions that you provide. Because of your position and role, you have the right to lay claim to others' energies, just as others, because of their position and role, have the right to expect something from you.

Consider some typical ways in which position and role might operate in a manufacturing company. Engineering, for example, might be responsible for developing a workable product. Manufacturing, for creating the product in a cost-efficient way. Marketing, for presenting the firm's product line in the marketplace. Sales, for persuading customers to buy the product. Quality control, for ensuring customer satisfaction with the performance of the product. Personnel, for staffing the firm with competent employees. Accounting, for making sure the firm's financial affairs are in order. And Data Processing, for maintaining suitable systems for managing the flow of information within the firm.

Each of the company's operating divisions and staff units would have the right and, for that matter, the responsibility to claim some of the energies of those in other work teams in order to get its work done. Sales, for example, would have the right to expect timely information from Manufacturing about how much time it will take to fill certain orders. Accounting has the right to expect up-to-the-minute fiscal information from Sales, Manufacturing, Quality Control, and other units without which it cannot keep track of the firm's financial status. Because it cannot do its work in isolation, each of the specialized groups must have the position and role to get what it needs from other groups within the organization.

Anyone who is familiar with large organizations knows that this is an idealized picture of how position and role works. The lines of both rank and responsibility are often questioned and disregarded. Divisions are often competitive with one another; they jockey for position, paying attention to their own work and ignoring their responsibilities to one another, and blame each other when things go wrong. This kind of competitiveness may be especially prevalent in a society like ours, which is founded on the basis of a deep suspicion of arbitrary authority. For whatever reason, in the United States, position and role by itself rarely serves as an effective channel for connecting energy.

Position and role works best when it's acknowledged by the colleagues and subordinates of the person who occupies the particular position and role. Many times people do not fully accept the right of office holders to lay claim to their energy. The legitimacy of a position in the eyes of colleagues and subordinates depends on three factors: (1) the credentials one brings to the office, (2) how one gets there, and (3) how one plays the role after one gets there.

The credentials one brings to the office. Depending on the office, credentials come in various forms. They involve a variety of factors, including family background, work experience, education, age, gender, race, and nationality. To hold office in hereditary monarchies, a person must be born into the role. Even today, offices in certain organizations are more apt to be open to those with proper family backgrounds and social credentials, such as a diploma from the right university. Familiarity with an organization and commitment to its purposes and values are persuasive credentials in many cases. Academic degrees, such as M.D. and Ph.D., also serve as credentials. Fortunately, recognized competence and the ability to do the job usually play a significant part in the acceptance of credentials as influential. An example of this follows:

Seventy-year-old Ted is the medical director of a county general hospital and a member of a prominent local family. Known as a "society doctor," he has an excellent bedside manner and is popular with his patients. Nevertheless, he is not so popular with his colleagues.

His fellow physicians consider him to be just short of incompetent because he doesn't keep up with new procedures, performs surgery that should be turned over to specialists, and records insufficient data on his patients' charts. New medical residents are advised to disregard his directives and to look for guidance from other physicians and from charge nurses.

Though in this case the legitimate authority of the medical director isn't challenged directly, it is circumvented. For his part, he seems content to hold a position that no longer serves as a connecting channel to the energies of colleagues and students. The fact that he is a physician does not give him the credentials he needs to earn the acceptance of other doctors. He lacks the skill and devotion to maintain his credentials by keeping up with new developments in medicine, which for physicians is essential.

How one gets there. The path one follows and how one is sponsored for a position play a part in determining how others feel about one's right to the office. It helps to be appointed by a well-established authority whose judgment is respected. It also helps to consult in advance the individuals whose cooperation is essential. Being viewed as someone who acted in bad faith, or who used trickery or deceit to achieve a position, will only hinder.

A widow marries her childhood sweetheart only six months after her husband's suicide. Her 11-year-old son and 14-year-old daughter, who weren't consulted about mother's remarriage, are upset. After a year of stormy battles and uneasy truces, the daughter runs away from home. A few weeks later the son is picked up by the police for shoplifting. Helped by court-ordered family counseling, the mother realizes that, in her children's eyes, she betrayed their father by marrying so soon after his death and betrayed them by not discussing remarriage with them.

Her second husband is not accepted as a legitimate stepfather because, in the children's eyes, he does not have the right to wear their father's mantle. He remains for them an illegitimate pretender to the father's throne.

How one plays the role after one gets there. Once office holders have been appointed, their legitimacy is either solidified or weakened by the actions they take. In any situation—be it family, working group, or social club—certain ways of exercising one's rights and responsibilities are acceptable, while others are not. The criteria for acceptability depend on attitudes and values that have become part of the culture of that situation. Gross violations of these norms upset those who identify with them, leading them to question the legitimacy of the office holder and to be less than wholehearted in making their energies available. Many factors, including social class, religious affiliation, and political orientation, affect how those in authority are expected to behave. In some circles, for example, corporal punishment is not considered legitimate, whereas in other circles, for religious or other reasons, people take seriously the adage "Spare the rod and spoil the child." In the United States, autocratic leadership is less legitimate in organizations today than it used to be and still is in more traditional societies. Participative management, which is more acceptable in the United States these days, remains suspect in those countries where subordinates expect bosses to tell them what to do.

A U.S. Army captain, who was a well-trained, experienced civil engineer in civilian life, is made commander of a combat engineering company. In only a few months, the company's performance goes downhill. Construction projects fall behind schedule, daily sick-call rates skyrocket, experienced noncommissioned officers ask to be transferred to other units, and two enlisted men go AWOL. Investigation reveals that the new commander has alienated both his commissioned and noncommissioned officers by criticizing procedures that they helped to develop and that they believe have worked well since the company was made operational two years ago.

The commander's criticisms violated his officers' strong sense of professionalism and pride in the procedures which they'd helped to establish. They are expressing their discontent by passively resisting the commander's leadership. They obey the letter but not the spirit of his orders. His position and role has not been established. Despite his rank, the outfit will remain in disarray until subordinates accept his right to command.

As these three cases illustrate, position and role can be challenged directly, resisted passively, or circumvented if those subject to that influence question its legitimacy. Though outright defiance is rare, passive resistance and indirect sabotage are not. It is the rare person who has not learned how to use delaying tactics, such as misunderstanding directions and obeying the letter but not the spirit of the law, as a way to question the legitimacy of someone in charge.

Coercion

Coercive influence involves using threats in order to get others to comply with one's wishes. The negative consequences of refusal or resistance may be physical, emotional, or financial, and they may lie within the law (e.g., threats of incarceration for drug use) or outside the law (blackmail). For an example of coercive influence, consider Tom and Jessica from the first case study in this chapter. Tom might easily have swayed Jessica's thinking by warning her about the guilt she would feel if she refused to help out an old and well-respected friend. If Tom had been a less gentle person or had felt belittled or degraded by Jessica's refusal, he or his community might even have threatened physical violence to back up his demand for the funds he needed.

Threat of punishment is the basis of coercive influence. Of course, punishment can take many forms. To some a tongue-lashing by one's boss may inflict as much pain as a whip-lashing. Confining a child to his or her room for an hour is coercive; so are the penalties of law. A teacher's belittling rebuke of a child before his or her peers is as humiliatingly coercive as was punishing people in colonial days by exhibiting them in the stocks in the town square.

Our willingness to be influenced by coercion depends upon the situation. We, the authors, agree that we would with alacrity hand over all of our money to a gunman threatening to shoot us. On the other hand, no amount of coercion would influence us to wittingly put our children or other loved ones in harm's way. What are the circumstances in which you might or might not accede to coercion?

Regardless of any personal or moral qualms you might have regarding coercion as a channel of influence, it is a possible channel for you to use as the basis for connecting with people's energies. Granted that by being punitive you may alienate others and create emotional distance between you and them. Still, it has its place. The normal Power Patterns of many people include resistance to being influenced by someone until they see that person is serious enough to invoke a threat. You in all likelihood have seen children respond in such a manner as well as adults, who carry such childhood patterns throughout their lives.

Obedience to coercive influence is built into our society and its institutions. The rule of law, in which you probably believe, is based on coercive influence. The right of employers to fire and demote workers for "due cause" is an expression of coercive influence. When a parent sends a child to his or her room to "think things over," the parent is making use of coercive influence. When you consider your own situation, you may discover that many times a day you either are subjected to coercive influence or are using it in your attempt to control somebody else's behavior.

Nevertheless, if coercion is to be successful, those whom you attempt to coerce must decide that it would be worse for them to resist your pressure than to go along with it. If, however, your intended victims decide to take the consequences rather than to comply, the use of coercion may no longer be sensible. You, too, must agree whenever coercion is attempted against you.

Reward

The use of the reward channel of influence involves our capacity to give something positive to others in recompense for their willingness to follow our influence. For our purposes here, we could say that a reward is a satisfying return on the investment of cooperation. Your successful use of reward as a channel of influence is, of course, predicated on your ability to produce the results promised, whether implicitly or explicitly, in return for cooperation. It is also predicated on the following five conditions:

1. Others must desire the positive result over which you have control.
2. They must realize that you have control of that result.
3. They must know that you are prepared to deliver that result if they comply with your wishes, and that you are prepared to withhold access if they fail to do so.
4. They must be able to comply, that is, they must have the ability to do what you want them to do.
5. They must agree that barter is appropriate considering the circumstances.

Unless all five of these conditions are met, any effort to use the reward channel of influence will be a waste of energy.

In the role of a result, a reward may be something as simple as the direct payment of money, such as cash for groceries or a bonus for outstanding job performance. It may be something as tangible as a new car, as symbolic as a gold star on a test paper, as personal as a hug, as significant as a long-sought-after promotion, as trivial as a celebrity's autograph, or as vital as an opportunity to discuss one's career plans with the president of the company.

Psychologist B.F. Skinner (1971) developed an entire science of shaping behavior based primarily on the power of reward. His studies demonstrate conclusively that if one immediately rewards an individual whenever he or she behaves in a way that one desires, it is possible to train that individual to do whatever he or she is capable of doing. In studies with rats, Skinner and his students rewarded his subjects with food whenever they behaved, initially by accident, as desired. After some number of such rewards, the animals would consistently behave in the desired manner. For example, they trained rats to climb ladders, carry American flags while crossing a tight rope, and perform other acrobatic feats on cue. After many such successful experiments, his methods have been applied to the realm of human behavior to teach mentally retarded individuals, to modify the behavior of severely disturbed, self-destructive children, and to induce convicts to behave in more socially acceptable ways.

You might find that Skinner's ideas have been widely received by business organizations. Indeed, certain writers on management have advised managers to adapt Skinner's reward approach in dealing with subordinates; for example, Kenneth Blanchard and Spencer Johnson, who co-authored the well-known book *The One Minute Manager* (1982). And many managers and organizations do use reward; formal or informal recognition, piecework rates, profit sharing, and merit-pay systems all make use of this channel for connecting employees' energies to corporate objectives.

Yet, even though it gets results, Skinner's approach has not been widely accepted. Why? In part because of the belief that employees are already sufficiently rewarded by their paychecks. If management were to offer them additional rewards, some managers feel, it would simply be bribing them to do what they should be doing anyway; therefore, seeking further influence via reward is unacceptable.

When we attempt to use reward, we may easily jump to incorrect conclusions about what other people want, or miscalculate how they will perceive our motives. On a flight from Bangor to Portland, Maine, a frustrated factory owner from Pennsylvania presented himself as a humanitarian entrepreneur. He initially boasted that he'd spent thousands of dollars improving rest rooms, cafeterias, and recreational facilities in a Maine plant he'd acquired a few years back. Later, however, he complained despite what he'd done to give his workers improved working conditions, their productivity had remained the same. He couldn't understand why his employees were so ungrateful and hadn't rewarded him with increased output for his efforts. In our view, this may be a case in which regional characteristics should have been taken into account—a case of miscalculation. The workers probably suspected that, as they might have put it, he "had an angle" for what he did, and Mainers and many others have in their Power Pattern a distinct distaste for and distrust of barters with "an angle," i.e., hidden agendas or unacknowledged motives. To use reward successfully, then, we must take factors such as these into consideration.

Expertise

The expertise channel of influence is based on the general notion that people who exhibit high degrees of knowledge and skill are valuable and deserve attention. To use expertise successfully, a person must either demonstrate ability in an area of value to others, or create the illusion of it; the determining factor is the *perception* that the person is an expert. Moreover, the respect that usually accompanies this perception affords the person a good opportunity to influence people's thoughts about matters that lie outside his or her recognized area of expertise. For example, our society traditionally values the thoughts and opinions of physicians even outside of the realm of medical expertise. We tend to respect "professionalism" in general. This is the essence of expertise as a channel of influence.

Two important caveats relate to influential use of the channel of expertise. They are:

1. The people to be influenced must perceive that you have expertise. People having direct experience of your expertise creates the most valid and permanent perception. Academic degrees (e.g., Ph.D. or M.D.), certifications (e.g., C.P.A.), and licenses (e.g., electricians and home contractors) are often useful initial substitutes for direct experience. Formal and informal references serve the same purpose. Occasionally, charlatans with no real skill, possessing only the trappings of expertise, are able to influence others through this channel. Influence gained in this manner is not only curtailed whenever the skill in question is needed or requested and cannot be demonstrated, but the perpetrator is often punished.

2. Someone must believe that you will not use your expertise to harm them in any way. Those with expertise as part of their Power Patterns believe that knowledge and skill *are* power, and could be used against them as well as for them.

The second condition can be especially problematic if you are dealing with people whose Power Patterns dictate that knowledge and skill *are in themselves* power and, as such, can be used against people as well as for them. These individuals have very mixed feelings about being dependent on outside experts, and they may feel diminished, one-down in their own power, when confronted by someone else's expertise. Thus, it is difficult to influence them through the use of expertise without first putting a lot of energy into winning their trust.

In general, the use of expertise is complicated by our society's love-hate relationship with experts. On one hand, we're often dependent on them, and this dependency, along with the perception that experts must necessarily be "smart," lends a certain mystique to them. For instance, the mystique of the physician is deeply ingrained in our Power Patterns, for we have been taught to trust our very lives to them and graduating from medical school is considered a remarkable achievement.

On the other hand, because we depend on experts so much, we often mistrust them. We license and certify them, insist that they live within certain ethical codes, and put oversight boards in charge of their work. At the personal level, we ask for second opinions, and refer to articles in *Readers Digest, Psychology Today, Consumer Reports*, newspapers, and other publications, so that our ignorance will not leave us totally at their mercy. We put experts in their place by such sayings as "Education is too important to be left in the hands of the experts." And deep down inside, many of us are convinced that, given half the chance, we'd do a far better job of teaching children, organizing health care, handling foreign policy, or dealing with any other area of expertise than those who are hired to do so.

As is the case with the other channels, you may or may not agree that this channel can influence you, that a perception of expertise—accurate or not—is sufficient reason for you to be influenced. Most of us, however, have been raised to have Power Patterns that hold expertise in highest esteem. Sometimes that esteem is well placed; sometimes it isn't. Where do you stand on this issue? What are your Power Patterns regarding expertise?

Attraction

Attraction as a channel of influence involves the willingness to be influenced by a person via a sense of personal identification with that person. Such attraction can take any of several forms, as follows:

1. The attraction may be rooted in and supported by a person's *prestige* or *reputation* for having a valued quality. Among the qualities that people typically value are achievement (Albert Einstein), notoriety (Charles Manson), integrity (Dag Hammarskjöld), good works (Mother Theresa), piety (Pope Paul XXIII), beauty (Elizabeth Taylor), athletic ability (Michael Jordan), or musical talent (Michael Jackson). Some persons are willing to be influenced in this way; some are not.

Do you have a valued reputation with someone whom you would like to influence? If you do, you probably don't realize it, for like many of us, you probably have a Power Pattern in which the ethic of modesty prevents you from acknowledging that you have a positive reputation.

2. The attraction may be based on a sense of identification with a group to which a person belongs. Ethnic-group identification, gender-group identification, and age-group identification fall into this category. Social organizations such as sororities and fraternities and service groups such as Rotary International and Order of the Eastern Star are also typical bases for this type of influence. The saying "Blood is

thicker than water" exemplifies why family should be put into this category as well. Whereas some persons can be influenced in this way, others cannot.

Are you a member of any group that is valued by a person whom you would like to influence? What about racial or ethnic bonds, your profession or occupation, gender, age, old high school or college ties, religious affiliation, or service club membership? All are possible sources of influence via valued group membership.

3. The attraction may be based on a sense of personal desire for intimacy. Such desire for intimacy might be based upon the other person's enthusiasm, tranquility, kindness, leadership style, or sexuality. Once again, some persons are willing to be influenced via such a sense of attraction; some are not.

Is a person you want to influence possibly attracted to you on a more personal level? Again, your modesty ethic might prevent you from knowing this, even if you feel it's OK to use such influence to your advantage.

4. Another source of influence via attraction is identification with important individuals in our lives, such as a parent, a sibling, a favorite grandparent, a "Dutch uncle," or a best friend.

Are you a favorite of someone whom you would like to influence more? Maybe, just maybe, it's OK to acknowledge such potential resources and even use them—for mutual benefit, of course.

5. Suppose you value someone in authority who seems older, wiser, and generally attractive as a person. It would not be surprising if you assumed that person's attitudes, values, behavior, and clothing style. It also would not be surprising if you were influenced by that person's thinking whenever you had to make a judgment about something, such as a request for help or a work-related decision. Prestigious persons and groups—TV and movie celebrities, political leaders, famous religious leaders, among others—often have great power of influence conferred upon them. Those of us who are in awe of their accomplishments will sometimes follow their lead when it comes to supporting worthy causes, taking a stand on social issues, and participating in political campaigns.

6. Finally, there are the ones we call *charismatic*. These are the people with whom we feel identification because they radiate self-confidence, a feeling of leadership, love for their fellow human beings, or other attractive qualities. The powerful flow of energy between them and those who admire and sometimes even worship them is based on attraction.

People generally have mixed feelings about the use of attraction as a channel of influence. On one hand, many people are downright skeptical and resentful when someone attempts to influence them simply on the basis that they belong to, or identify with, the same social group as he or she does. Others are often suspicious of people whose only credentials appear to be their reputation or public image. And they fear that the followers of charismatic people give their leaders the power to exploit them and do great harm.

On the other hand, many people are quite comfortable with this channel of influence and are open to using it and responding to others' attempts to do so. They feel a special bond with those who belong to the same social, religious, political, or ethnic groups that they do, as well as with those who are like them in age, gender, sexual orientation, or some other important way. They might rely on a person's reputation and cultivate their own reputations in other peoples' eyes. The powerful positive flow of energy that radiates from certain charismatic individuals inspires them to make changes in their lives which they otherwise would not have made.

Many of us, if not most of us, would do virtually anything within reason (and sometimes beyond it) for those we care deeply about and who are important to us. Family, friends, mates, children, and other loved ones could be included here. And as many of us have Power Patterns shaped in part by a history of having been badly betrayed, and hurt from such relationships and, therefore, no longer will allow ourselves to be so influenced.

What are your Power Patterns in regard to attraction? Do they work well for you, or have you limited yourself in this area?

Group Solidarity

The group solidarity channel of influence is based on our feelings of commonality and kinship with whomever works toward the same goals as we do, holds the same values as we do, or fights against the same enemy as we do. For example, consider again the first case in this chapter. To sway Jessica's thinking, Tom might have said, "Look, Jessica, we've stuck together as friends for a long time now. And we're working toward the same goal, the revitalization of our town here, and my diner in my part of town would go a long way towards that revitalization. We've got to fight off these outsiders like McDonald's and the other chains that want to come in here with big-city management styles that none of us want! Now, what do you say? Let's keep our town in our own hands!"

Such use of common goals, common values, and common enemy could have been quite appealing to a local banking official and an old friend. Such appeals would work under the following conditions:

1. The person being influenced must recognize the commonality of goals, values, or enemy on which your appeal is based.

2. Those goals, values, and enemy must be important enough to evoke enough emotional energy that the person accedes to your wishes or at least continues to negotiate with you.

Group solidarity contributed much to the success of the civil rights movements in this country, providing fortification in the battles against racism and for women's rights. Many strange bed-fellows banded together across race, sex, and class lines to work toward the common cause. Group solidarity at the national level is critical for the success of war efforts. Witness the difficulties the United States suffered during the Vietnam War because of the lack of national solidarity. In World War II, the solidarity of the Allies primarily (the United States, Great Britain, France, and the Soviet Union) was greater than that of the Axis powers (Germany, Italy, Japan, and other nations). That differential was a major factor in the ultimate success of the Allies.

• The United States probably would not have reached the moon as soon as it did if not for the national reaction to the U.S.S.R. launching the first manmade satellite, Sputnik 1.

- Organizations that have a strong esprit de corps—such as I.B.M., Delta Airlines, and 3M—often have greater success and face adversity better than do companies with less loyalty.

- Many people will go to self-sacrificing lengths to help out a family member in trouble, regardless of any personal animosity.

- Many members of social or service organizations will allow themselves to be influenced by total strangers once their common membership is discovered.

- Estranged husbands and wives will often stay together for "the good of the children."

Skeptics might tend to apply the pejoratives *parochialism* or *insularity* to group solidarity as a means of influence. They might also see it as antithetical to the high value we place on individualism. Others, like Tom, might pass up a perfectly useful channel like group solidarity because, given their Power Patterns, it might seem like "imposing" on someone— something a person shouldn't do.

How do your Power Patterns relate to group solidarity as a channel of influence? Have you been aware of its possibilities? Are you currently involved in a situation in which it might be useful to you?

Networking

The essence of the networking channel of influence is respect for the usefulness that can occur via a set of informal, interconnected relationships. The amount of influence within any particular network is dependent upon the size of its informal membership and the positions held by its members. The larger the membership, the more multitalented and far-reaching is its influence. The higher the positions represented in the network, the greater the impact its influence might have.

Access to a network is made through a "contact." Contacts are members of a desired network who might either influence a decision on your behalf or pass you on to another member in the network who might be able to do so. This brief case study is an illustration of gaining access to a network.

You have a new degree in engineering and are looking for a job. It is common knowledge that many people do not get jobs through newspaper ads, but through "contacts." Fortunately, your spouse has a close friend (Evelyn) who works as an accountant in a civil engineering firm. Your spouse agrees to speak to Evelyn, who in turn suggests that you call the director of personnel and mention her name to him. The personnel director says that there are really no appropriate jobs open at this time, but he suggests that another engineering firm, with which they do a lot of work, is looking for someone with your qualifications. He picks up the phone, calls his counterpart, hands you the phone, and an interview is scheduled right there and then. In fact, you get the job.

In this case, at least three overlapping networks were used: the friendship network, which included the spouse and her friend, Evelyn; the organizational network, which included Evelyn and the personnel director; and the professional network, which included the personnel director and his counterpart in the hiring firm. Each of these individuals were willing to be "contacts" and were influenced by the value they perceived in their network. This willingness is essential to networking and, as in this case, usually not difficult to find. Many people will agree to be used as network connections because of the long-term probability that the network will someday be of personal use to them; others will agree because they enjoy the status that often goes along with being a member of a particular network.

Networks have one primary rule for their members: Help out other members as best as you can. This help might include talking with a stranger at the request of a network member, passing the requester along to someone who might be better able to help, or simply dispensing honest, sincere advice. Also, in general, to use networking as a channel of influence, the person you wish to influence must either be a member of your network or must sufficiently value your "contacts" with your network.

Unfortunately, some networks have a secondary rule that says that people who are not like the current members may not avail themselves of the benefits of the network. For example, "old boy" networks are famous for their ability to influence important decisions regarding organizational, civic, and government policy. They are also infamous for their exclusivity which traditionally has kept females and non-whites out of their pervasive circles of influence.

Mentoring is an important aspect of networking. The younger people who are new to a field or organization don't know its rules, Power Patterns, or key players. Many flounder around for a while and either learn the rules the hard way, get stuck at a middle-management level, or move on. A lucky few are picked as proteges, however, and are given a mentor. Ideally, the mentor not only contributes to the protege's professional skills but, more importantly, also guides the young person through the labyrinth of organization pitfalls and makes available the all-important network of contacts and connections.

Michael met Don in one of Don's classes at Johns Hopkins University. For whatever reason, Don saw a lot of potential in Michael and took him under his wing, so to speak. In doing so, he gave Michael the benefit of working under his tutelage for several years, as well as the benefit of being introduced to members of the professional power structure as someone worthy of their interest and support. Without Don's mentoring, Michael may have eventually achieved the success that he currently enjoys; still, Don's sponsorship and tutelage was priceless.

Ironically, during Michael's initial year as a student in Don's class, he had no idea of Don's networking influence nor of Don's interest in him. Mentoring generally works from the top down, rarely from the bottom up. Mentors choose proteges, not the other way around. If you want to choose someone to mentor you, you might enhance your chances of being chosen if you find out which channels of influence that person is amenable to, and then use them. In this case, Don was open to the channels of expertise and attraction, and Michael used them well without even knowing he was doing so.

Many people reject networking as a legitimate means of using or garnering influence. Such people usually prefer to be valued for themselves—for their personal expertise or attractiveness—rather than for their connections to others. They believe that influence should be earned through hard work, diligence, and "what you know" rather than "who you know." Others interpret networking as "brown-nosing" and, according to their Power Patterns, inappropriate.

What do your Power Patterns have to say about networking? Do they approve of using networking as a channel to connect the energy of others with yours? When is the use of this channel appropriate? Inappropriate?

The Function of Congruence

The seven channels of influence, whether single or in combination, are effective only when they are congruent in some way with the beliefs, or Power Patterns, of those whom you seek to influence. In the previous chapter we spoke about the belief systems or lessons that instruct us how to go about influencing other people and when we will be influenced. These lessons lay out in our minds the acceptable and safe paths to follow when we're trying to get the results we want. We may or may not find these lessons personally agreeable; however, they do determine which channels of influence each of us will use in attempting to influence and deciding whether or not to be influenced. For example, most of us would not like the idea that we would do what an authority figure tells us to do simply because that person is an authority figure. Still, many of us obey our bosses and parents for only that reason. For any particular channel to be effective, the person being influenced must perceive that channel as congruent with the lessons of appropriateness and efficacy that are a part of our Power Pattern.

Role and Position. In the case of role and position, congruence means that those you seek to influence via your position accept that you have the legitimate right to claim their time and energy for specified tasks. For me to influence you via position power means that you must agree with my right to influence you because of the role you occupy in relation to me.

Coercion. In the case of coercion, congruence means that anyone you seek to coerce physically, emotionally, psychologically, or legally is willing to comply with you rather than face the negative consequences with which you are threatening them. For me to influence you via coercive power, you must see the potential of my threats as more costly than letting me influence you.

Reward. In the case of reward, congruence means that the person you want to influence has concurred with you that barter is an appropriate and effective way to be influenced. Without that agreement, you might offer that person something that he or she values highly but will not accept. A much-in-debt police officer turning down an offer of cash because he or she is not open to bartering traffic summonses would be a good example of disagreeing with the reward channel of influence.

Expertise. In the case of expert power, congruence means that whomever you seek to influence values expertise as an appropriate channel of influence in and of itself and perceives you as an expert. For example, for us to influence you via expertise, you must value expertise as an appropriate channel of influence in and of itself and perceive us as experts. We have Ph.D.s in psychology. Because of the expertise implied by our degrees, some people would take to heart our recommendations regarding economics as well as psychology. Others would only pay attention to our ideas on psychology. Yet others would find virtually no meaning at all in our degrees.

Attraction. In the case of attraction, congruence means that others feel a sense of identification with you and value you because of it. For me to influence you via attraction, I must exhibit some quality that you can personally identify with. This makes me a worthy person who deserves you as a loyal ally, companion, or follower.

Group Solidarity. In the case of group solidarity, congruence means that others feel a close bond with you as a member or leader of their group. For me to influence you via solidarity power, you must identify with me as a fellow group member who is joined with you in a common cause.

Networking. In the case of networking, congruence means that others are prepared to accept and use you as part of a web of interrelated people that is important to them. For me to influence you via network power, I must be able to connect you with network members who, in your eyes, are significant potential resources or allies.

Standards of congruence concerning which channels are acceptable differ from one culture to another. Within the United States, the kinds of agreements that are possible in any situation depend a great deal on the social and subcultural backgrounds of those involved. People often do not see eye to eye on how they should or should not go about trying to influence others. Not only do ways to influence others differ from one society to another, they also tend to change with the times.

For an example of how acceptable channels differ from one society to another, and from one era to another in any single society, take the coercive use of public humiliation. In the People's Republic of China during the Cultural Revolution, it was acceptable for patriotic young people to parade, in the streets, teachers and other so-called "traitors" of the revolution, wearing dunce caps and placards describing their "crimes." It was also common to hold sessions of public criticism in which those accused of having betrayed the revolution were expected to analyze their mistakes and admit the error of their ways.

Many Westerners vehemently disagreed with these methods of using power. Horrified by such public sessions, they argued that these were nothing but outrageous violations of human rights. In China, however, the idea of moral self-criticism was not invented by radical Communists. It goes back thousands of years and is a respected way of, as the twelfth-century Chinese philosopher Zhu Xi put it, "wiping the dust from the face of an old mirror so that it shall be once more bright" (Clayre, 1984, p. 39). In other words, it is quite possible that the humiliated victims themselves were "in congruence" with the methods being used, even if they felt they were being unjustly accused.

Although many people in the West considered the use of such humiliating treatment to be barbaric, beyond the pale of the civilized West, they had only to glance at the mirror of history to find similar treatment in use in their own countries. Colonial Americans who offended the community were frequently confined by the head and limbs in stocks in public squares so they could be scorned and ridiculed by fellow townspeople. Not very many years ago, in American public schools, naughty or "lazy" children were punished by being made to wear dunce caps and sit on high stools in the front of the classroom. Moreover, even today the public confession of one's sins or moral shortcomings is an accepted practice of certain religious groups in this country and is one of the steps required of alcoholics by Alcoholics Anonymous.

Within a complex society such as ours, beliefs about what influence channels should or should not be used will differ from one section of the country to another, from group to group, and even from one person to another. Consider the world of business in contrast to the world of friendships. In the former expertise is a highly valued channel of influence whereas attraction is not. In the latter attraction tends to be more valued as a mode of influence than expertise. Followers of B.F. Skinner's ideas about behavior modification are more accepting of the use of rewards to motivate students or workers than are those who believe that people should do what's expected of them without having to be "bribed."

Because people in our society come from so many different backgrounds, it is a mistake to assume that there is agreement between you and others regarding acceptable ways of attempting to influence people. Everyone does not have the same ideas about the right and wrong ways to go about using power. You cannot be certain, therefore, that an energy channel will be acceptable in someone else's eyes just because it appeals to you. This is true whether you're on the giving or receiving end of an influence attempt.

Agreement about energy channels is not always direct and overt. It's possible for you to use a channel to get what you want even when you're not aware of using it—so automatic is that part of your Power Patterns. We call such a connection "covert agreement." Quite commonly, a parent will unintentionally use the energy channels to steer a child into studying for occupations in which the child has little interest. The channel that the parent is unconsciously using may be the position channel (the child obeys because it was Father's wish), the attraction channel (the child loves Mom very much and wants to please her), or coercion (the child obeys because he or she fears loss of approval). The parent was using the channels of influence and directing the child's energies even when not aware of doing so!

Covert congruence has both advantages and disadvantages. On the plus side, it means that it is possible to establish an energy channel with others even when they're not fully aware of what's going on. In this way, unnecessary confrontation is avoided, peoples' cherished beliefs remain unchallenged, and, on the surface at least, there is harmony and cooperation. On the minus side, covert agreement can be wasteful. Sometimes it takes time and energy to figure out covert signals. For example, when Don was executive director of a community mental health center, it took time and energy for his staff to figure out what he wanted when he wasn't being direct. Covert agreement also opens the door to confusion and frustration when people misinterpret what is wanted. There were times, for example, when Don's staff mistook for directives his requests for their opinions on a particular course of action. As a result, they thought they were carrying out his wishes when, in fact, they were not.

What is acceptable is certainly relative and moral judgements need not apply to the channels of influence. However, when used from the finite perspective of power, any channel can be used exploitatively or oppressively. In the situation of those publicly humiliated in China, the social acceptability of such behavior may have been thin cover for propaganda if the coercion was supposed to yield truth. Children, all too often, yield to sexual abuse through the use of the position channel. High-ranking Nazi leaders exploited the channel of group solidarity extolling the need for purity in the Aryan race, while influencing German soldiers to implement the "Final Solution" of exterminating the German Jews. These Jews were often obeying their authority figures as, when told to by their leaders, they boarded trains to the death camps. Chapter 7 goes into more depth about this issue as it explores power and the problem we have made of diversity.

The bottom line is this: When we are fully conscious of our Power Patterns, we can with full awareness choose whether or not we wish to be influenced, and thus avoid being victimized. When we pay attention to the Power Patterns of others, we give ourselves the opportunity to use any or all of the channels of influence to support them in using their energy on our behalf.

CHAPTER FIVE:

POWER AND EQUITY

At this point, let's assume that you are clear about a goal and want to achieve it. In fact, you want so much to achieve it that you have set your plans in motion and are actually working toward the accomplishment of that goal. Since you can't achieve the goal by yourself, let's also assume that you have influenced another person, through an acceptable energy channel, to use her or his energy on your behalf. This connection proves helpful as you continue working toward your goal. Then, after you've invested a lot of time and energy and are well on your way there, the other person begins to balk at going further with you. What's going on?

HOW CAN INFLUENCE BE MAINTAINED SO THAT IT IS SATISFYING AND PRODUCTIVE FOR BOTH PARTIES?

This next phase of the Energy Model of Power describes the dynamics of maintaining your influence with such connections so that they will continue to use their energy on your behalf. We call this phase Equity. To maintain influential relationships, a sense of mutual Equity is necessary. The higher the sense of Equity we experience, the higher will be the satisfaction; the lower the sense of Equity we experience, the lower the sense of satisfaction.

Equity as Fair Exchange

People will continue to help you achieve your goals if they feel that you are reciprocating as much valuable energy as they are giving, i.e., that there is a fair exchange of energy on behalf of your goals and their goals. Although in theory fair exchange may seem simple, in practice it is often quite complex. To illustrate, let's take another look at the case study that opened Chapter 4, in which Tom applied for a loan at Jessica's bank.

Suppose Jessica and Tom had taken full advantage of all the energy channels available to them. What kinds of fair exchange might have appealed to them? What did Tom want? What did Jessica want in return? And, did Tom have it within his power to give Jessica what she wanted?

Tom wanted enough money to start a business. Jessica had control of that money and could have loaned it to him if she felt justified in doing so. In return, Jessica clearly would have had sufficient Equity if Tom could have assured her of his ability to repay the loan. There were also other possibilities, however, about which Tom remained unaware.

He had far more resources to offer in equitable exchange for the loan than either he or Jessica realized. For example, Tom could have offered the satisfaction of helping out an old childhood friend. He might have persuaded his friends, fishing buddies, and fellow parishioners to increase their business with the bank. He might have spoken positively about Jessica's willingness to back his business venture, thereby boosting her reputation in county and state political circles.

Both Jessica and Tom limited themselves by their preconceived ideas about what is and is not a "fair" exchange of resources in a business transaction. It never occurred to Tom that his ability to affect the bank's business and Jessica's reputation could be a legitimate part of a fair exchange. Therefore, these Equity chips were not available to Tom even though they might have made a significant difference to her.

What can we learn from what went on and did not go on between Jessica and Tom? First, we see that questions of equity and fair exchange almost always involve issues that have to do with people's ideas of right and wrong, that is, they involve social standards or personal rules that all of us follow to some degree. We use these internal yardsticks to determine what is fair or not fair in the energy exchanges between ourselves and others. They tell us what we should or should not offer to others in exchange for their efforts on our behalf. Similarly, they tell us what we should or should not accept from others in return for our decision to align our energies with theirs.

Values

The desire to remain true to our values in our dealings with others lies at the center of this matter of equity. These values give meaning to our lives and are integral to our sense of self-esteem. We use them to guide our activities with images of what is right and desirable (we pay for goods rather than steal them). We use them to lend coherence and predictability to the way we think and behave (such as the dependable and satisfying give-and-take of successful marriages). We use them to justify our actions and attitudes (I neglected my family when my boss promised to give me a bonus if I could bring in the ABC contract within the month, *or* I quit when my boss offered me a bribe for looking the other way).

Sufficient Return

In addition to questions of whether or not it's proper to use certain resources, there are also considerations regarding whether we are getting enough in return for what we give. We feel angry and hurt when we consider that we're facing bias, unfairness, or injustice directed against us. We're more apt to respond wholeheartedly to others' requests or demands if we feel we're being treated fairly than if we feel we're on "the short end of the stick." In an infinite game of power, it should not be hard to find out whether a fair exchange is possible in any situation. All that's required is for everyone to lay their cards on the table.

The first step is for both parties to be clear in their own minds about what they want or need. Second, both parties reveal what those wants or needs are. Third, both parties become clear in their own minds about what each is willing and able to offer the other. Fourth, both parties communicate clearly what they are prepared to offer in return for what they want or need.

When we play the game of power finitely, however, it is often difficult to work out an exchange of energies or resources that satisfies both players. A lot of time, effort, energy, and tough negotiations usually are needed to establish a fair exchange of resources, since "getting the short end of the stick" is something that happens to losers. The energy drain of protecting our self-esteem is clearly an issue.

Knowing Our Needs and Communicating Them

Whether we play the game from a finite or infinite perspective, it is important for the players to be clear in their own minds about what they want. We've repeatedly noticed how difficult it is to be clear with ourselves about what's really at stake. For example, I ask for respect when what I really want is only someone to listen to me; or, I ask for more attention from you when what I really want is to know that you still like me.

Why is it difficult to arrive at such clarity? Often the simple fact is, we just don't take the time to ask ourselves what it is we really want— what genuine hopes and needs lie hidden under the mask of our demands. This kind of question requires a willingness to confront one's own needs. Underneath our surface demands are wishes and concerns about which we feel uncomfortable and more vulnerable than we would like. This is often the case in instances where we want reassurance that we are right and approved of, that our competence is appreciated, that we are liked or loved, or that we're still in control. These aspects of ourselves have to do with our personal pride and self-esteem. They involve two strong desires—to avoid feeling humiliated, betrayed, or put down, and to avoid having to admit defeat. We fear that if we acknowledge and ask for what we want, we would make ourselves vulnerable to humiliation and defeat.

This is why we often are uncomfortable about asserting ourselves. We don't like to make our wants known to others and often resent outspoken people who do not hesitate to tell others what they want. One way to minimize our discomfort with self-assertion is to remain vague and unclear in our own minds about what it is we want. Thus our desires remain unspoken and unclear to ourselves as well as to others.

Comic routines have been built around the idea that certain needs should be satisfied without a person having to express them directly. The classic situation involves the complaint to a spouse, "You never tell me you love me." When the spouse replies, "Of course I love you!" the response is, "That doesn't count. I had to ask. If you loved me, I wouldn't have to ask." Many times we wish our loved ones or associates at work would recognize and respond to our unspoken needs. Rather than express those needs directly and run the risk of appearing to be "needy" in others' eyes, we choose to live with frustration and disappointment. It's the rare person who feels comfortable saying to bosses, subordinates, or colleagues, "I thrive on appreciation and recognition. Be sure to tell me when you think I've done a good job."

Often we don't make our wants known clearly and directly because to do so doesn't fit our ideals about the kind of person we *should* be. We *shouldn't* impose on others. We *shouldn't* be "pushy," "selfish," or "controlling." And we don't want others to think of us in these ways. We often feel better about ourselves if we are keeping the peace, bending over backward to make sure that others like us, and helping others get what they need even *when it doesn't seem fair to us.* This is the classic "you win/I lose" perspective in which I find myself angry and resenting you because you are not meeting my unspoken wants. Eventually I will repay you in kind, either openly or covertly, for your unfairness.

In the infinite game of power, the successful exchange of energy and resources is facilitated when players let one another know what they want and need. Doing so is easier in the infinite game because the risk of loss of face, disapproval, or threats to our self-esteem is minimized. In the infinite game we do not put those currencies at stake. The very purpose of the infinite game—the win/win mutual maintenance of each other and our relationships—requires such openness. A successful energy exchange also depends on our finding out what the stakes are for all the players. Playing infinitely, we have no qualms about asking the other, in effect, "What kind of outcome do you want for yourself in this exchange?"

Under the win/lose conditions of the finite game of power, however, several factors stand in the way of our finding out what the other side wants. First of all, it often doesn't even occur to us to ask. We take it for granted that others will tell us, or we assume we know what they want based on our past experience with them, others like them, or what we would want if we were in their place. Then we act on these assumptions without realizing that they may be partially or entirely wrong.

Individual Perceptions and Equity

By the time we're adults, most of us have discovered that life doesn't always seem fair. We've reconciled ourselves to that fact and figured out ways to deal with it that are not offensive to ourselves or others. Some of us, however, have arrived at less moderate ways of doing so. At one extreme are those people who feel OK about aggressively going after what they want. They see life as a jungle. They don't hold back, waiting for others to be sensitive to their needs. They're willing to claw and struggle in the jungle of life. They're clear about what they want, know that others may be going for the same prize, and will fight for what they want because they believe that "nice guys finish last." For them, virtue is *not* its own reward.

At the other extreme are altruists. They want to satisfy others' needs and to contribute to the greater good, even if it means giving up some other personal desire. They choose the option usually known as self-sacrifice. Some may think that these people give more than they get. However, they are getting what they want—the pleasure of making someone else happy. For them, "virtue is its own reward." Both the jungle fighters and the altruists, those who are aggressively self-assertive and those who consistently appear to be sacrificing their self-interests to respond to others' needs, are being true to their beliefs. They are going after what for them is fair exchange.

Most of us fall somewhere between those two extremes. We accept the fact that life is sometimes not fair. We realize that it often rewards virtuous behavior with nothing else but the inner satisfaction of having done what was *right* or what we *should* do. Sometimes it's possible for us to feel that there is fair exchange in the old adage, "Virtue is its own reward." At other times, however, we feel let down and bitter if the only reward for doing the *right thing* is self-satisfaction. Down deep, we prefer to reap more tangible benefits for responding to others' desires.

Many of our power struggles involve differences in beliefs about what an equitable return is. In his negotiations with Jessica for the business loan, Tom might have offered Jessica the satisfaction of helping out an old friend. She might have thought that was inequitable, not a sufficient return for her to grant the loan. They might have easily engaged in a power struggle over the value of such a suggestion. He might threaten to have his supporters withdraw their deposits on the grounds that racial bias influenced her decision to deny the loan. She might have seen that as *very* unfair. A major power struggle could have ensued over that. When either party considers himself or herself *right* about what is fair and equitable, including being *right* about having been inequitably wronged, power struggles easily begin. As we are willing to attend to each individual's definitions of equity, we stand a greater chance of coming to an infinite, win/win resolution.

Equity and Currency

Low Equity Relationships

Sometimes we resign ourselves to living with situations that for various reasons we feel unable or unwilling to change. In some cases, the possibility of greater satisfaction simply does not come to mind. However unsatisfying, unfair, or downright unjust a situation may seem, we are often resigned to it—it's always been this way and is a normal part of our lot in life. In other cases, such unsatisfying situations are thought of as the lesser of evils. We often hesitate to give up these relationships because of the minimal equity provided by our hope for greater satisfaction in the future. Also, because there are real or imagined dangers in letting go of an unsatisfying relationship, we may settle for less than the satisfaction we would like. To use an old saying, we "make the best of a bad bargain."

We use the term *low equity* to refer to making the best of a bad bargain. We feel stuck with what we have and accept it, although we are basically dissatisfied because our inner needs are going unmet. This dissatisfaction may be expressed from time to time, but it is never not strong enough to lead to change. Are you involved in any low equity relationships? With whom?

Typical examples include:

- Disgruntled employees who stay on the job for years in order to collect retirement benefits, even though they dislike or resent the work for which they're being paid.

- Spouses who stay together "for the kids" or because "this is better than nothing," even when all love and happiness has long since disappeared.

- Physically and emotionally abused wives who remain with their husbands because they're afraid they cannot support themselves and their children on their own.

- The many citizens who, knowing that certain actions of elected or appointed officials are corrupt, say, "You can't fight city hall!" —by which they mean that they feel helpless to do anything about it.

- The poor and homeless who, though bitter about what life has to offer them, seem resigned to their fate and see no way out of it.

Any time we are in low equity relationships, a great deal of our energy goes into dealing with frustration and anger—either our own or the other person's. The chronic stress of pain and disappointment saps our ability to effectively use our energy intellectually, emotionally, and physically. We confirm our helplessness with our inability to figure a way out of our dilemma. Even the desire to do so can dwindle to the point where it is too feeble to make a difference. The situation seems hopeless. This is apathy.

We know, however, that apathy often is a cloak for anger and resentment, even rage. Cloaked as apathy or not, such anger and resentment stimulate action toward another form of equity—the equity of mutual pain, "tit for tat." It is not unusual to find a low equity relationship in which the energy exchange is based on a vicious circle of behavior aimed at causing as much pain as has been received—the vengeance system of "an eye for an eye, a tooth for a tooth." Covert acts of sabotage or flare-ups of impotent anger are common among those who settle for low equity energy exchanges. At the extreme, the anger erupts into violence, resulting in physical injury, murder, suicide, or riots including fire-setting, looting, and the general destruction of property. These eruptions are clear indications of the extraordinary amounts of energy that can be bound up in unsatisfying low equity relationships.

Fortunately, there is a more effective way of dealing with low equity relationships. It calls for us to focus our energies fully upon moving toward high equity through (1) asking for what we want, (2) asking what the other person wants, and (3) negotiating toward mutual satisfaction. These are explored more fully in Chapter 8. If such negotiations are not successful, ending the relationship altogether and finding other ways to get what we want is clearly the course of choice.

What we need to establish are high equity relationships. These relationships involve an exchange of energy or resources that truly satisfy all concerned. There is a genuine sense of fair exchange. Though compromise *may* be involved, no one feels short-changed or cheated. As a result, energy flows freely and is directed to agreed upon purposes.

Currency of Exchange

Understanding the basic types of currencies exchanged in the management of equity is useful if we are to increase our ability (1) for what we want and (2) find out what the other person wants.

The term *currency of exchange* has been used for many years to describe the various kinds of resources that are used to establish equity in the game of power. The standard definition of *currency* is "a medium of exchange." As it's being used here, currency is anything that has positive value for someone. It's hard to imagine anything on earth that under one set of circumstances or another would not be valued by someone. Just think, for example, of the craze not so many years ago when perfectly sane people paid good money for "pet rocks"! Basically, then, the nature of what might be exchanged is limited only by what people value and by what they're willing and able to make available to one another. Theoretically, the possibilities are limitless.

We offer a six-fold typology of currencies of exchange adapted from a system developed by Uriel and Edna Foa (1974) in their important work on exchange theory.

The six basic types of currencies of exchange include:

1. Money
2. Tangible goods
3. Intangible services
4. Positive regard
5. Prestige
6. Sexual gratification

Money. This is what usually comes to mind when we hear the word *currency*. Every society today uses some type of legal coinage and paper note as a medium of exchange for goods, services, or the payment of debts. Although rates of exchange usually differ from one country to another, money has a distinct advantage over other forms of currency because it can be exchanged for virtually any kind of commodity; the only requirement is that a person has enough money to meet the set price of that commodity, be it goods or services.

Tangible goods. These include the many thousands of natural or manufactured items in the world that people in various settings and circumstances feel they want or need. These goods may be useful (e.g., food, clothing, housing, tools) or decorative (e.g., jewelry, art); readily available or scarce; designed for a specific purpose or applicable for many purposes; useful to only a few or valued by large numbers of people; prized for what they symbolize (e.g., trophies) or desired because of the high cost of the materials with which they are made. All that matters in any situation is whether the items in question are valuable, for whatever reason, in the eyes of those we wish to influence.

Intangible services. Here, too, there are literally thousands of services that people around the world value and offer others. These services may be relatively abundant or scarce; they may be the kind that virtually anyone can provide, or they may depend on highly specialized knowledge and skill; they may be necessary to maintain life and well-being (e.g., medical care, teaching, legal services), or they may be nonessential ways of catering to people's comfort and ease of living (e.g., housekeeping services, buying services.) Once again, all that matters in any situation is whether the services in question are valued, for whatever reason, by those we wish to influence.

Positive regard. Positive regard includes romantic love, friendship, familial affection, such as the feeling of a parent for a child, and caring based on religious principles. Positive regard may have to do with nothing more than the empathy one feels for fellow human beings. It may be based on a specific, intense relationship between two people, or may spring from the gratitude or admiration people feel when someone has acted on their behalf. It may also arise from what psychologist Carl Rogers called *unconditional positive regard*, by which he meant the deep sense of appreciation that we often feel for those we are close to, regardless of occasional disapproval of their behavior. Obviously there are many reasons for expressing positive regard for someone else, and many ways of doing so.

Prestige. This refers to the reputation enjoyed by a person who, in the estimation of others, counts for something. Titles, one's name on the office door, people's deference and respect, and many other signs, symbols, and benefits of high status are all part of the currency of prestige. Virtually every society has ways of honoring valued members in special ways. Every organization in this society has its own particular hallmarks of status and prestige for outstanding members. There are many elements that, singly or in combination, can lend prestige to a person: social or cultural background; familial or social link to others of high standing; personal accomplishment; the exhibition of personal integrity, such as having passed a rigorous test of values and beliefs; field of knowledge; extent of experience, whether in a professional or personal context; and superficialities such as social manners and style of dress. The acceptance and respect expressed by one's peers is a sign of prestige, as is the deference expressed toward a person by those on a lower rung of the social ladder.

Sexual gratification. Sexuality and power often are associated with each other. Though sexual politics in the workplace are often looked down upon, sex is used to achieve positions of power in organizations and to influence those in positions of leadership. Like money, sexual favors can be exchanged for any of the other currencies of exchange. Unlike money, however, which can be exchanged by anyone who has it, regardless of who they are or what they look like, the use of sexual gratification as a currency of exchange usually is limited to those who meet certain criteria of beauty and sensuality.

Finally, currencies of exchange are often used to represent something else more directly related to our pleasure or survival. Money, for instance, always represents something else—the ability to purchase tangible goods or intangible services and possibly to secure prestige, self-esteem, or power itself. Currencies such as approval, recognition, love, and respect often represent our self-esteem.

When we view power from the infinite perspective, it is easier to recognize the energy patterns, i.e., Power Patterns, that lead us to see others as the source of our self-esteem and approval. We must beware of assuming that others can give us the intangibles that we more readily can, and responsibly should, give ourselves. Such an assumption only misdirects our energy, driving us into attempts to exert our influence over others so they will fully meet our expectations and provide for us. It is best if, at the start, we realize that no one else can ever give us sufficient quantities of money, prestige, control, approval, recognition, love, respect, and the like, if we confuse our desire for those items with our desire for self-esteem, self-approval, and self-respect. In many ways, we are actually relinquishing power to others when we believe the degree of our self-regard is necessarily dependent on how highly others regard us. Such errors of thinking are born of the finite perspective of power and tend to keep us in never ending power struggles. From the infinite perspective, we can take back our rights of approval from those who would withhold such approval and use our energy to approve of ourselves.

CHAPTER SIX:

DISEMPOWERMENT: HOW AND WHY WE PLAY THE FINITE GAME OF POWER

Why do we get stuck in power struggles? The information in the foregoing chapters is not new, nor is it particularly difficult to understand. Why, then, do we so often feel so powerless? The reason has to do with the countless ways in which we, singly and together, fail to take charge of our lives, fail to focus and unleash our energy so that we accomplish what we want, and fail to experience the productivity and satisfaction that is available to all of us. The term we use for such failures is *disempowerment*.

As we have emphasized before, all human beings are born with the energy of life at their disposal. We begin life with more than enough energy to accomplish whatever we want. Notice how a small child reacts when he or she has a strong desire for a cookie or toy that's just out of its reach. The child knows what he or she wants, backs it up with strong emotional conviction, and goes for it with complete body, mind, and spirit. We do not lose this energy.

By the time most of us are grown, however, we have learned to limit the ways we commit our energies to achieve our aims. We are less vigorous in our attempts to get what we want. We restrain the fullest possible use of our minds, our emotions, and our bodies. We block the expression of our potential talents, often denying that this potential ever existed in the first place. We scatter our energy in fruitless attempts to reach many different objectives at once. We reject or overlook possibilities for connecting our energies with others who, if approached from their frame of reference, might become effective allies. We make adversaries and even enemies by failing to understand or appreciate others' views of what is fair, just, and equitable.

In other words, in every part of the Energy Model of Power—energy conversion, harnessing, and exchange—we disempower our "selves" by failing to tap into the incredible amount of energy that is at our disposal. Disempowerment is the inevitable result of playing the game of power in a finite way. In the finite approach to life, we make rules that we feel *must* be obeyed. These rules set boundaries within which we must play. Every game has a beginning and an end. It ends when someone wins. And, when someone wins, it is because someone else has lost.

HOW WE LEARN TO PLAY THE FINITE GAME OF POWER

In our society—and as perhaps has been the case for people in most cultures of human history—as we grow from unrestrained, fully empowered children into more restrained, mature adults, we learn to play the game of power in a finite way. We do this in at least two ways. First, we learn that there are different rules for different situations. For example, while it may be acceptable to demand something from a sibling or peer, demanding something from a parent or a school teacher would likely result in punishment of some kind; however, later on, when we enter the workplace the compliant, passive approach, which got results in school, may have to be given up in favor of a more assertive, competitive stance. Once we realize that each game has its own set of finite rules, we begin to develop the ability to find out what the "real" rules are in each new situation. And as we all know, some people are far more skillful at using informal contacts at the water cooler and elsewhere to figure out what are the real rules.

Second, we establish a set of rules for ourselves and other people that define the kind of players we ought to be. Through countless experiences—first with parents, then with teachers, peers, and innumerable other people—children begin to figure out what others expect of them. They start the lifelong process of developing a "self" that is designed to deal, for better or worse, with the demands and expectations of others. This is the process of socialization. Consequently, what people often refer to as "self" is nothing more nor less than the set of rules that every individual develops to reinforce the kind of player he or she is, or to delineate the kind of player he or she ought to be, in the finite game of power.

The Lessons We Learn and the Rules We Set

Experience taught us many lessons when we were children. One of the first things most of us learned was that adults often disapproved when we were too outspoken about what we wanted. They treated us in a loving way when we expressed our "selves" moderately and scolded or punished us if we became too insistent and forceful. And so we learned to hold back—hold back our thoughts, hold back our feelings, and hold back our movements. We also soon learned what it was like to be helpless and dependent on others for love, protection, food, and the basic necessities of life. It didn't take long to decide that sometimes it was better to settle for half a loaf than to insist on the whole thing and risk our basic well-being and even life itself.

In the process of learning such lessons, we came to the conclusion that we weren't always going to get what we wanted, no matter how strongly we felt about the situation or how vigorously we expressed ourselves. We experienced the painful frustration of wanting something desperately, only to have it refused. Because the pain was so unbearable, we taught ourselves to modulate our desires, to experience our wants less intensely, and to settle for less, oftentimes, than what we really wanted.

And so we curbed our passions and set rules about who we were and how we should behave in order to survive, be loved, and be cherished. We learned to place finite limits on the use of our infinite energy, that is, we decided:

1. To minimize or denigrate our goals and desires by being acceptably unclear and tentative about those goals and desires

2. To place the comfort of others ahead of our own by neither experiencing nor expressing the full strength of our passion

3. To minimize the risk of disapproval by rarely committing ourselves fully to our goals either in speech or in action

Disempowerment is inevitable when we play the game of power in such finite ways. The rules that define "self" are designed to keep us safe and out of trouble. Such rules also rule *out* many other ways in which we could use energy to influence others and work out equitable exchanges that would benefit us. They place limits on what we allow our "selves" to do. How many times have you heard yourself or someone else say, either boastfully or regretfully, "I'm not the kind of person who. . . "? Perhaps the rule and limitation has to do with the use of intellectual energy—"I'm really dumb when it comes to mathematics." Perhaps it has to do with the energy of emotions—"I would never wear my heart on my sleeve." Perhaps the energy of the body—"I'm just too lazy to exercise regularly."

The rules about who we are or ought to be also limit the possible ways that we allow our "selves" to connect our energies with others, i.e., to influence others. It is possible, for example, to rule out the use of every one of the seven channels of influence on what appear to be justifiable grounds. Position as a channel of influence can be rejected because "it's not possible to be a boss unless one exploits the workers, and I don't want to exploit anyone." The coercion channel can be rejected because "the use of force of any kind is morally wrong." The channel of expertise can be rejected because "it weakens the fabric of society if people become dependent upon experts." The channel of reward can be rejected because "it's wrong to bribe people for doing work they should be doing anyway." The attraction channel can be rejected because "that's how tyrants like Hitler or Jim Jones are able to dominate and destroy." The group solidarity channel can be rejected because "group-think is never as courageous and effective as the work of a single creative individual." Networking as a channel of influence can be rejected because "name dropping and brown-nosing destroy morale in an organization."

Finally, the rules we set for our behavior can limit our options when it comes to working out equitable energy exchanges that enable us to get what we need from others and, in return, give others what they need. At one extreme, as self-protection grows into paranoia, suspicion and mis-trust can poison our ability to negotiate fair exchanges. At the other extreme, the need to be self-sacrificing and to avoid feelings of guilt often hampers our ability to assert our desires and, consequently, makes it difficult for others to know what they can do to be helpful.

There are innumerable ways in which rules about our and others' behavior can interfere with our ability to focus our energy, to influence others, and to develop high levels of equity. All too often, we end up in persistent power struggles, burdened by anger or depression that wastes our energy, and fail to achieve desired results for all concerned.

WHY DO WE CONTINUE PLAYING THE FINITE GAME OF POWER?

If the finite perspective of playing the game of power is so disempowering, why do we continue to play it? To gain some understanding of what's involved, it's necessary to take a closer look at how the "self," which plays such an important part in defining the rules by which each of us lives, is created. Then, we will describe what happens when we perceive this "self" as real and take it so seriously that we attempt to protect and enhance it. We will also examine the so-called "not self" or "shadow"—those rejected aspects of "self" that often go unrecognized but which, nonetheless, affect what we think and do. Finally, the three "psychic furies" of guilt, shame, and humiliation often associated with the "not self" or "shadow" will be explored.

Creating the "Self"

When we speak of "self" we mean the awareness that each person has of being a separate and distinct individual who exists over time and has certain qualities and characteristics that distinguish him or her from all others. From the time we are born until the time we die, each of us is busy creating and verifying those qualities and characteristics. Freud and others have described in some detail how we have lots of help in this process of self-creation—first from our parents and other caretakers, and later from a great many other people. They present us with many rules, guidelines, norms, and values. Some of these we incorporate as our own and some we reject, according to whether they work or don't work in the circumstances of our infancy and early childhood. What worked and didn't work depended to a large extent upon how the people around us reacted to our efforts to try out different ways of being and behaving. They applauded some, punished us for some, and greeted some with indifference.

With all of this help, *we* made crucial decisions about which personal qualities and rules we would use to define and describe both who we are and who we would ideally like to be. We become, in other words, creators of ourselves. And in the final analysis, we still are—we are playwrights and novelists creating and devising our "selves" as characters that can be as complex as Hamlet, Electra, Antigone, or Oedipus. In truth, we are far more creative than Shakespeare, Sophocles, or any other writer in creating our "selves." Unlike the playwright or novelist who creates a character for a single play, each ordinary person creates a "self" that is able to perform in an unending series of life situations and can improvise responses at any time of day or night with neither script nor prompter.

We work hard and put a great deal of energy into maintaining, refining, and defending this character called "me" that we have created over a lifetime. We take our "selves" seriously. So seriously that most of us have long since forgotten that we are the authors of our identities. Thus we have also forgotten that we can edit, rewrite, or otherwise change the script of our "selves" and our lives.

Two Fundamental Themes

Let's look at two fundamental themes with which our scripts or stories must deal. They are *When am I safe?* and *When am I in danger?* Our stories about these issues are essential to our survival and help explain why the human race has dominated the planet. Psychologically, these stories determine our sense of self-esteem—the evaluations and judgments we make about our worth as human beings.

From the moment we were born, our parents and others responded either positively or negatively to us depending on what we were doing. When we were praised, cuddled, fed, and stroked, we felt safe, good, and at one with our "selves" and the world. Inevitably, however, we had to deal with times when our feelings of self-worth were shaken and endangered by disapproval—harsh words, disciplinary action, refusals to give us what we wanted, and perhaps even physical punishment and ostracism.

At first such disapproval came as totally unexpected and could be devastating. Rarely were we entirely clear about what we had done to deserve such treatment. Neither were we entirely sure that we would ever again return to a state of feeling safe and good about our "selves" and the world. Accordingly, we created stories about our "selves" and the world to make sense of these attacks and to design defenses to deal with them. Younger children have no way of knowing what is really going on. Accordingly, the stories they create are as much fiction as fact.

Creating one's "self" can be as fraught with anxiety and feelings of impending danger as taking a walk through an uncharted minefield. Because of these not unusual feelings of extreme danger, the stories the small child creates about these incidents are "as reality." They pervade our assumptions about the world and persist through time to become a part of our adult "selves." Though often forgotten superficially, these stories are easily reactivated by real or imagined threats in the adult world. This occurs even though the responses called for by these stories were invented for the world of the child and probably are inappropriate for an adult world. Thus the "self" may be likened to a piece of light, buoyant cork floating on a sea of anxiety, valiantly doing its best to remain above the surface but occasionally being flooded by unexpected waves that wash over and threaten to submerge it.

Under such circumstances, it's not surprising to note that we do our best to protect our "selves" from all possible threats to our self-esteem. We cling to strategies and images that have served us well in the past. We insist on playing by the rules of these stories that have brought us to this point in our lives, despite all anxious moments, failures, and frustrations. Playing the finite game is the best way we know to survive, to keep our heads above water, and to protect our "selves" against possible disaster.

Creating The "Not Self"

To further our understanding of why we play the finite game and how we continue to disempower our "selves," let's take a more in-depth look at how the mind works. The mind, as the noted Harvard philosopher Susanne Langer (1957) has pointed out, is the organ system whose job is to create distinctions or ideas and to make choices based on those distinctions. Just as the heart pumps blood, the lungs oxygenate the blood, and the stomach secretes digestive juices, the mind takes note of differences, makes generalizations, and performs the job of distinguishing one set of qualities from another. Anyone who has meditated knows that it's next to impossible to quiet the mind entirely. Even when we don't want it to do so, the mind continues to do its job of creating ideas and distinctions. Even in neutral, our mental motor is still running.

An idea is a mental image that organizes our experience. It brings together qualities or characteristics that seem to belong together, that fit into patterns with which we are familiar from the past. To make a distinction involves identifying an idea in such a way that it is separate and *distinct* from other related qualities or characteristics that are *not* that idea. For every "this" there must be a "*not* this." For example, the idea of "chair" must include the idea of "not chair." Within the distinction "not chair" lies the idea of "table," an object which for the most part we do not sit on as we would a chair. The idea of "up" makes no sense without the contrasting idea of "down." "Good" cannot exist without the concept of "bad," "moral" requires "immoral" or "amoral," and "right" requires "wrong."

By the same token, there cannot be a "self" without a "not self." For every quality one uses to describe "me," there is always a corresponding "not me." If you consider yourself "smart," then your corresponding "not me" might be "stupid." If I am "rational," then I am not "emotional"; if "determined," then not "half-hearted"; if "hard-working," then not "lazy."

Many of our "not me's" consist of qualities we would not like to have. Suppose you prefer to describe yourself in such terms as *tough, controlled, discriminating, hard working,* and *rational.* You would probably be very uncomfortable seeing yourself as a "bleeding heart," or as "impulsive," "unprincipled," "lazy," and "over-emotional." Suppose you would prefer to describe yourself in such terms as *caring, spontaneous, tolerant, laid back, expressive.* You would most likely not be comfortable being perceived as "selfish," "up-tight," "judgmental," "driven," and "cold." We do not enjoy seeing our "selves" or being seen by others as our "not me's."

Notice that in some ways one person's "self" may resemble another's "not self." Whereas the first maintains a self-image that is self-protective, controlled, discriminating, hard-working, and rational, the second rejects an image of "not self" that is selfish, up-tight, judgmental, driven, and cold. In the examples above, my "self" and your "not-self" do resemble one another. However, the connotations are very different. The first set is slanted positively and the second negatively because they reflect judgments that we make about whether or not the traits are acceptable, given our stories about how we should be.

Therefore, you might label me as "selfish," "up-tight," "judgmental," "driven," and "cold," but I would probably reject those labels. I reject them even though they refer to the same basic traits that I call "tough," "controlled," "discriminating," "hard-working," and "rational." Similarly, being caring, spontaneous, tolerant, laid back, and expressive are positive qualities with which you identify. Being excessively sympathetic, impulsive, unprincipled, lazy, and overemotional are negative qualities that I reject.

Two things need to be understood here. First, each quality of "me" cannot exist without a corresponding opposite, and usually devalued, quality. Second, even though we would like to do so, these negatively valued characteristics can neither be avoided nor rejected; because the devalued "not self" has already been created within our minds, it is an inescapable part of us. To get a firmer grasp on these ideas, and to see how the "not self" is a potent factor in our tendency to disempower ourselves, it is helpful to view this side of us in Jungian terms, as one's *shadow*.

The Power of the Shadow

However hard you may try, you cannot avoid your "shadow self." Although it usually remains out of sight and buried in your unconscious, it is always there; it goes wherever you go. We are uncomfortable with our shadow. As we were growing up we were scolded, punished, ridiculed, and put down for behaving in unapproved ways. Such ways have become, in time, our shadow—our "not me." In other words, we associate our shadow traits with pain, and when confronted by the threat of experiencing such pain again, we feel anxious and therefore eager to avoid the danger.

Note well that every shadow quality we reject as bad or undesirable can be given a positive connotation. "Bleeding heart" can become "caring"; "cold" can become "rational"; "driven" can become "hard-working"; "overemotional" can become "passionate." It is also important to note that positive characteristics also live within our shadows. If my story about myself is that I am selfish, dumb, or otherwise worthless, then in my shadow are the helpful, smart, and worthwhile qualities of me.

In either case, we use an extraordinary amount of energy suppressing, denying, and vehemently defending against our "not me's," our shadow. At the same time, we use a like amount of energy to prove, verify, corroborate, and justify our "me" stories. This is critical to understanding how we disempower ourselves. If we were to accept the "shadow self" as not only real, but also valuable, we would, as a consequence, increase our sense of power in the following ways:

1. We would be aware of the lessons we've learned in the past and the rules we've set to deal with those lessons. This would enable us to make, using our *full* repertoire of experience, conscious choices about how we will behave. Our full repertoire of adult experience holds

many revisions to our shadow lessons about what is safe and what is dangerous that are much more appropriate to our current life.

2. We would have the flexibility to use our "shadow self" as well as our "created self." If, through awareness, I do not limit my behavior to that of my "smart self" which is often driven to prove its "smartness," I can become even smarter by availing myself of my "ignorant self" which longs for learning.

3. We would no longer spend so much of our energy and power denying our "shadow selves" and defending our "created selves" on behalf of our self-esteem. Accordingly, we would have much more power available to achieve whatever goals of productivity and happiness we may have.

The Three "Psychic Furies"

There are three major "psychic furies" that are associated with the pain of our disempowerment:

1. Guilt
2. Shame
3. Humiliation

We experience *guilt* when we believe we have done something wrong or immoral. Guilt is a negative judgment we've learned to impose on ourselves. It is triggered when we feel we have behaved in ways that our stories about our "selves" tell us are wrong or otherwise unacceptable and *shouldn't* be done by one's "self." Feeling guilty, we easily might justify our unacceptable actions by thinking or saying, "I wasn't being myself," or "The devil made me do it!"

Shame is the feeling we experience when we believe that something we have done either is overtly subject to disapproval and ridicule by others, or would be subject if others knew about it. Shame is triggered when we experience *who we are* in ways that our stories say is wrong or otherwise unacceptable in the eyes of others and *shouldn't* be a part of one's "self." When we are ashamed, our actions are unjustifiable, and we cannot find a way to excuse ourselves.

We experience *humiliation* when we believe that what we've done or who we are is publicly scorned or ridiculed by others whom we see as being better than we are. Under the circumstances, we feel helpless and unable to justify our "selves" or our actions and feel powerless to defend ourselves. The sense of humiliation is well reflected in the homily "It is better to keep your mouth shut and have folks think you are stupid, than to open your mouth and prove that you are stupid." Substitute any word that fits for *stupid*.

The Pitfalls of Collective Identity

The force of humiliation, though commonly recognized by people and used by storytellers since the time of the early Greeks to drive plot and character, has not yet been widely recognized in Western psychology. To understand humiliation, we must understand an additional, highly important fact about the "self": that the "self" not only includes an individual's personal definitions of the "self" but also embraces, and in many ways depends on, identifications we make with groups of people who are like us. We call this the *collective identity*, in contrast to the *personal identity*, which refers only to the unique characteristics of the individual. The collective identity is, of course, shared with other people.

Everyone's sense of "self" is connected to a number of collective identities. We are all of the following: members of families; men or women; black, white, Asian, or members of some other racial group; Catholic, Protestant, Jewish, agnostic, atheist, or followers of some other religious belief system; members of the middle class, the working class, or another socioeconomic group; American or citizens of some other country; child or adult; young, middle aged, or elderly. These are some of the ways in which we identify our "selves" with large numbers of other people and enlarge our sense of personhood with a feeling of significance in a social context. Depending on how we're viewed and treated in that context, we can confirm the rules we already have for how to play the game of power (as we generally do), we can alter the rules, or we can worry, feeling anxious, powerless, and confused.

We try hard to protect our "selves" from the three psychic furies and the psychological pain of recognizing our "not self." We must, however, inevitably experience the guilt, shame, and humiliation that is associated in our minds with experiencing or expressing those aspects of our "selves" that we have decided are unacceptable. Moreover, no matter how hard we try to avoid the stigma of being identified as a member of a group that is held in contempt by others, there is no escape from assaults on our collective pride. Consider, for example, how vulnerable Americans were to the experience of humiliation when Iran took over the U.S. embassy and held our diplomats hostage.

Whether our "psychic furies" derive from judgements associated with our personal identities or our collective identities we, too often, spend inordinate and disempowering amounts of energy feeling guilty, ashamed, and humiliated. Our mighty efforts to deny such feelings are just as disempowering. These feelings are useful when they prevent us from behaving in the future in ways that harm ourselves or others. Unfortunately, they too often occur when the only harm that occurs is the harm to our sense of self-esteem, OK-ness, and power.

As we have said already, the "ought's and should's" of our rules or stories about ourselves and life determine how we play the game of power at each stage in the Energy Model. We use these rules and stories to place limits on (1) how we convert the energy of life for use intellectually, emotionally, and physically; (2) how we attempt to influence others in our behalf; and (3) how we attempt to maintain an equitable exchange of energy and resources with those with whom we must collaborate. By perceiving the limitations of the finite game as "reality," we disempower ourselves. When we follow the rules we set for ourselves, all too often we overlook opportunities for using our energies differently, to the fullest extent possible, and in ways that increase the probability of influencing others in ways that are mutually beneficial.

The question, therefore, is not whether the rules should be relaxed or improved; it is whether or not paying the cost, in energy and power, to continue engaging in finite power struggles and reinforcing familiar but devaluing self-perceptions is worthwhile. We think not. Playing the game of power by finite rules neither empowers us nor protects us from psychological pain. No matter how hard we try to defend our "selves" against expressing the "not self," it is always part of us and is being expressed whether or not we notice. And no matter how hard we try to throw away the parts of the "not self," they return; it is as if we were throwing boomerangs.

Consequently, we do not really make much progress in either our inner or outer world when we play the finite game of power. We raise the same defenses again and again, and often find ourselves doing or experiencing exactly what we swore we would never again allow to happen. How many parents, for example, have found themselves doling out the same treatment to their children as they received when growing up, despite vows never to treat their own children that way? Again we see the process of *boomeranging*. It is a common occurrence in the life of anyone who plays the finite game of power.

This chapter might lead one to believe the ways we disempower ourselves are inexorable. And given the stories from our friends and colleagues, in books and on television, plus our own experience; there may be some truth in the statement. However, we can remedy much of our disempowerment and help others do the same. In fact, this is the purpose of this book. Following the promised chapter on influence and the problems of diversity, we do describe how to mitigate, if not reverse, our tendencies toward disempowerment. In Chapters 8, 9, and 10, we describe the actions of empowerment, how to discover the excellence that is within us all, and offer specific suggestions on how to make empowerment work. In Chapter 11, we explore how to empower others.

CHAPTER SEVEN:

INFLUENCE AND THE PROBLEM OF DIVERSITY

In Chapter 4 our discussion of the seven channels of influence focused primarily on influence at the interpersonal level. As these channels can also help us understand the dynamics of oppression in our society and in its organizations, and as understanding these dynamics is important to us if we are to play the infinite game of power, in this chapter we will view the channels from a new angle. Our emphasis will be on how the channels have been used as tools of oppression and how oppressed groups have used the same channels to empower themselves in their struggles for social justice and organizational equality. The discussion will focus primarily on women and people of color, yet it could equally be concerned with religion, social class, and sexual orientation.

OPPRESSION AND THE SEVEN CHANNELS OF INFLUENCE

In Western society, white males fall into a category whose members have traditionally had within their grasp much more power than women and people of color. We saw in Chapter 1 how differences are used to determine who wins and who loses. We saw how society has traditionally assigned "winner" to male and white and "loser" to female and people of color. Accordingly, those in the white male category have been able to dominate virtually all channels of influence relative to females and people of color. Their control over those channels made it possible for them to dominate organizational and social policymaking, determine priorities for allocation of funds and access to information, and, in various ways, limit other groups' access to needed resources.

Some students of oppression would make white males the villains in the piece. However, that is a disempowering perspective which does little more than suggest a finite restructuring of who wins and who loses. Starting with the Emancipation Proclamation in 1863, proceeding to the successful women's suffrage movement of the early 1900s, and continuing into the civil rights acts of more recent times, our legal system has intentionally and progressively weakened, though not abolished, that domination. A more effective perspective is derived from looking at today's problem as a present-day collusion strongly reinforced by pervasive socialized belief patterns from the past. These belief patterns are about the supposed insufficiency of women and people of color as compared to white men. This perspective, however, is complicated by the growing, but still incomplete, esteem that women and people of color have been cultivating about themselves over the past 100 years. This complication often results in the repression of the still operational belief of insufficiency coated with growing, but still incomplete, gender-and race-esteem. When women and people of color with such belief patterns encounter a white male with the same belief patterns in his organizational domain, they often display Power Patterns that include counterdependence, prideful deference, and passive aggression. Such Power Patterns create confusing, non-productive, and still losing, situations. Unavoidably, white male dominance of the channels of influence continues, and the prophecy of the belief pattern of insufficiency has thus fulfilled itself. Fortunately, the '80s and '90s are producing more and more young people without the conflicting messages of insufficiency and esteem, allowing them greater access to their full power.

Position and Role

In the past, few people who were not white and male were allowed senior positions and roles of authority, whether in government, business, or nonprofit human service organizations. Today those who occupy such positions are still primarily white males, although a small and growing trickle of women and minorities is finding its way into top leadership positions. With few exceptions, women and people of color play subordinate roles, minimizing their opportunities to use this channel of influence.

Despite the growing recognition of this disparity and efforts to close the gap, social norms and expectations still prompt teachers and counselors to guide female and minority children toward career choices that do not prepare them for senior positions which control resources and make policy. As even the parents of these children may hold lower expectations for them, it's not surprising that the children themselves have a limited view of future possibilities in life.

White males say that the doors of opportunity to these positions are open. These doors are capable of a wider opening, and women and people of color must notice their own collusory and debilitating belief patterns. These belief patterns cause partially opened doors to appear closed. Women and people of color must be alert to *any* collusory and debilitating belief patterns they may be carrying, and do their best to free themselves of such patterns.

Coercion

Dominant groups in any society use many different ways to keep other groups powerless and second class. Our traditional organizational cultures demand that employees conform to the patterns of speech, dress, socializing, and other general behavior of the dominant group. If these informally enforced patterns are not followed, promotions do not occur, raises are not received, or hiring does not occur in the first place. Many organizations point with pride to the several women and people of color in their executive ranks as proof of their will toward diversity. However, in too many cases, a not very close inspection yields strong evidence that those women and people of color speak, dress, and, in general, behave like their white male colleagues. If any of these new entrants to the executive suite were to revert to the cultural behaviors of their own groups, their tenure as executives would be short-lived.

Coercion is the real or perceived threat of sanctions, whether they be psychological, financial, physical, or of some other type. For example, as was widely reported in the press during and following the 1991 Senate hearings over the appointment of Clarence Thomas to the Supreme Court, even the most highly educated professional women hesitate to report instances of sexual abuse on the job for fear that their careers will be jeopardized. Repeated studies show that a sizable proportion of rape victims do not go to the police because of their unwillingness to face humiliating interrogations, physical examinations, and court appearances.

Ironically, as women and minorities began to close ranks in the struggles for civil rights, coercion became the single most effective channel of influence with white males. The coercive tactics of sit-ins, economic boycott, and other tools of passive resistance, as well as the violence of rioting, eventually led to recognition by those in power that business as usual was no longer possible. As a result of the civil rights movements, legally assisted coercion is now in evidence as white males open their organizations for fear of severe losses to their public images and corporate pocketbooks.

Just as individual women or people of color fail to use the protection of the law, some white male managers overprotect themselves by refusing to use appropriate disciplinary measures with employees who fall into a "protected" category. Such actions on the part of either party simply reinforce the problems.

Rewards

"He who has, gets" is an expression that applies here. Having been in positions of power for generations, white males and the institutions they control have amassed immense economic resources, which are used, in turn, to reward those who cooperate with them. Jobs, promotions, information, juicy projects, and pay raises go to those who support the goals of those who control those jobs, promotions, information, juicy projects, and pay raises. Similar rewards are used to influence elected officials and public opinion. Women and people of color are dependent upon these rewards for their livelihoods while having not nearly the same quantities of reward to offer on behalf of their own goals.

Equal pay for equal work is a high-sounding slogan that, despite legislation to support it, still is far from being practiced in the marketplace. Throughout the nation's business firms and nonprofit organizations, such as universities and social agencies, female employees often are not paid the same as men who do similar jobs. Despite so-called "quota systems" for employment and promotion, equally qualified African Americans are less apt than whites to be hired and promoted in many organizations.

Because they have amassed, as mentioned above, far less wealth than their white male counterparts, women's groups and minorities have far fewer rewards to use in influencing elected officials and in getting their message across to the general public via the media. Changes are taking place, however. Efforts have been made to develop financial institutions dedicated to increasing the economic base for women and minorities. Laws giving special advantage to minority owned firms seeking government contracts represent additional attempts to enlarge the reward channel for these groups.

Meanwhile, substance abuse and other social problems grow like mushrooms in our cities. Young African Americans, feeling cut off from the rewards of well-paying jobs, good educations, and the respect of society at large, seek rewards from other sources. Promising young men with talent and initiative become affluent drug pushers; equally talented and promising young women settle for prostitution or single parenthood at an early age. The vicious circle of crime and poverty associated with blocked reward channels continues from one generation to the next.

Again, are the doors of economic opportunity really open, or are women and people of color simply not walking through those doors? As in most cases the answer to either question is probably both "yes" and "no." Certainly better educational, social service, and mental health systems would open the doors of opportunity wider in our inner cities. At the same time, many opportunities are passed up because of insufficient belief in the self, a situation that can only change when individuals change from within.

Expertise

In the past, those who were not white and male did not have equal access to education and training as a matter of law and custom. Denied the opportunity to gain technical knowledge and skill, how could expertise become a viable channel of influence for them? Today, the paths to knowledge and skill are legally available to all, but often without the economic resources needed for many people of color to move very far along those paths. There are still many corporate managers who automatically assume that women are inherently incompetent in any technical discipline. Consequently, women are often not accorded influence from the highly respected channel of expertise, regardless of any credentials they might have, such as degrees in engineering or physics. Likewise, those same corporate managers often assume that many people of color, regardless of documented experience, do not have the skills to rise very far up the corporate ladder. Even with appropriate education, training, and experience, women and people of color are still denied full access to the expertise channel of influence.

The situation has begun to change in some respects. Women are entering medicine, law, and the executive suite in ever greater numbers. They are trickling into such male bastions as engineering and military leadership; however, the leadership of these "male" disciplines remains largely in white male hands. African Americans, too, have gained greater access to previously all white professions. There are outstanding examples of black men—including Supreme Court Justices and military leaders—whose influence in the public arena is based on their command of the expertise channel.

Several decades after the historic Supreme Court decision calling for desegregation of public schools, however, we are faced with the tragic fact that the education of the vast majority of young persons of color fails to provide them with the skills and knowledge needed to wield the channel of expertise. An estimated 40 percent of them drop out of high school. Many of those who do graduate are, according to many reports, functionally illiterate and unable to deal with everyday arithmetic. Writing in *The Washington Post*, 3 November 1991, Dennis Goodman, a substitute teacher in a high school considered to be one of the best in Washington, D.C., reported that absenteeism ranged between 38 and 50 percent, and that students were passed from grade to grade regardless of what they had learned. "Reading, writing and math skills were so poor that a case could be made for devoting the entire sophomore year to remedying those deficiencies." He concludes:

> Academically, these young people have been cheated by their families, by government, and by the people who control their education. Most disturbing is that these students seem to have no idea of how far behind they are. They view a passing grade as a sign of satisfactory work, not realizing that the standards against which they are judged are distressingly low. (p. 3)

Again, the answers are the same: the systems must improve, and people of color must empower themselves to demand those improvements and, when necessary, to avail themselves of the minimally integrated, white systems that do work.

Attraction

Generally, the culture of the corporate world does not see the attraction channel of influence as operable. However, successful women have been and still often are accused of "sleeping their way to the top." In this negative manner, some women have been allowed influence through the channel of attraction. Physically attractive women have been able to get "public" positions (receptionists, flight attendants, models, secretaries) in areas where less attractive women were not allowed. This channel has not been useful to "unattractive" women and people of color (who have been generally seen as unattractive) in the working world. At the same time, many studies have documented that physically attractive white men are more successful than those who are considered less attractive. Women and people of color do not naturally possess the "attractiveness" of the white male "look"; they are not white males and cannot possess such attractiveness, regardless of any attempts they may make to win via the emulation of others.

Has this changed? Is more change needed? Yes, to both questions. The numbers of physically attractive people of color seen on television are certainly up. Yet there may be a shortage of truly charismatic leaders, as was Martin Luther King, Jr., and a range of media figures that extends beyond super athletes and entertainers would be welcome. Hillary Clinton, however, is arguably a major breakthrough for women in the area of charismatic leaders.

Group Solidarity

Although rarely aware of doing so, white males have bonded together in tight-knit groups around athletics, the stock market, and other "manly" interests such as hunting and fishing. Members of the "old boys' clubs" called only upon one another to recruit new employees and to develop new enterprises. Until recently, these male preserves were off limits to females and people of color. Exclusive clubs and drinking establishments reinforced white male solidarity. In these places, and in this manner, business was conducted and information and resources shared. Remnants of this exclusivity can still be found.

By the 1960s, and usually in reaction to living on the fringe of white male groups, females and minorities were making effective use of the group solidarity channel in their struggles for recognition and equality.

Black Power groups began to educate themselves and young African Americans about their own history and culture. In consciousness-raising groups, women helped one another recognize and confront ways in which they were disempowering themselves by accepting traditional, subservient roles.

Fortunately, there were also many whites who were attracted to the cause of civil rights and added their weight through broadened group solidarity. Similarly, many men have supported and found value in identifying with the cause of women's rights. At the same time, this is a channel that women and people of color could use much more intensively. The power of large numbers of people in solidarity has long been recognized as a *very* effective channel of influence.

Networking

The dominant position of white males was for generations maintained by the existence of "the old boys' club." This "club" comprised far-flung networks of successful white males that cut across industries and national boundaries. Informal referrals over drinks, on the golf course, and within other white male bastions were the means by which younger men gained access to those in power and learned how to make use of connections to gain their economic, political, and social objectives. Of course, the networking channel was closed to women and people of color.

Along with the use of group solidarity, however, came the discovery of the importance of networking as a channel of influence for oppressed people. Today in large businesses and government agencies, there are formal and informal networks of women and African Americans who, though they are employed by the same or related organizations, do not work directly with one another. In these networks, members find mentors and learn how to survive, protect each other, and get things done in their organizations.

Judging from what we observe in our consulting work, a growing number of previously exclusive white male networks are opening to women and minorities. Networking promises to become in time a major influence channel for exploration of diversity, resolution of differences, and elimination of oppression.

The problem of organizational and social oppression based on the finite tactic of withholding access to the channels of influence, though improving slowly, is still with us. The challenge is to do the paradigm-shifting work of using the infinite perspective of power. Then, and only then, will our organizations and communities begin to use differences for their inherent value as a source of learning. Consequently, the channels of influence will be used as tools to build the diverse partnerships needed to make our organizations more productive and our communities places of well-being for all citizens. Used finitely, the channels will continue to be coin-of-the-realm in the game of win/lose as differences continue to be used to determine who is winner and who is loser—making losers of us all in the long run.

CHAPTER EIGHT:

THE ACTIONS OF EMPOWERMENT

The goal of those who play the infinite game of power is to keep the game going by ensuring that everyone is winning in the long run. It's a game of infinite possibility in which everyone has the opportunity to become their best and to discover new areas of growth and talent. When we are taking advantage of these opportunities, we call this the empowerment game. We define empowerment as those acts of supporting people, whether ourselves or others, in self-discovering and acting upon their own inherent excellence.

THE THREE ACTIONS OF EMPOWERMENT

The actions of empowerment are as follows:

1. **Focusing**—the use of our intellectual energy to consistently and persistently make our own choices regarding how we want to live our lives.
2. **Being Passionate**—the focusing of our emotional energy on our chosen goals so that we will put ourselves into motion toward those goals.
3. **Acting**—the use of our physical energy to pursue our choices regarding how we wish our lives to be. In a sense, acting powerfully is the result of focused passion.

Our intellects, our emotions, our bodies all operate best when used passionately in focused action. If we constrain our energy in any of the three forms, our ability to use them atrophies from disuse, and such misuse can cause the malaise of apathy and mental and physical illnesses. Empowered, we allow our energies to flow, and in that flowing we experience productivity, satisfaction, joy, and well-being.

Focusing: the Essence of Intellectual Empowerment

Empowered, we are able to think clearly by (1) taking in all the relevant data available, (2) sorting the data into useful distinctions and patterns, (3) discerning fact from our own assumptions, and (4) setting goals and making decisions that will be effective in both the long and short run. Empowered, we spend less time and energy in confusion, not knowing what to do, or in conflict over what to do. Because we are clear and focused, we know what we want and stay engaged in the process of getting it—enjoying both the process and the result.

The Impediment of Conflict

One significant impediment to being well focused is conflict. Conflicts occur when one is confronted by goals that appear to be mutually exclusive. They can be approach-approach conflicts—wanting two things that seem mutually exclusive; for example, wanting to complete two projects of equal priority that have the same deadline, wanting a new car and a vacation, or "wanting to have your cake and eat it too." There can be approach-avoidance conflicts—wanting one aspect of something while wanting to avoid another aspect of that same thing; for example, wanting to ask the boss for a promotion but not wanting to appear self-serving. A third form is avoidance-avoidance—wanting neither of two options, one of which it seems must be chosen ("the lesser of evils" syndrome); for example, not wanting to reject (for fear of losing business) a major client's request that you replace an African-American account executive with a white one because, in the view of the client, "Negroes always have difficulty working with our culture" and not wanting to compromise your organization's new diversity policies and your personal integrity.

In any of these conflicts, if the relative emotional strengths are about equal we will vacillate and experience frustration and increasing anxiety until the goal of wanting to get rid of the frustration and anxiety assumes enough priority to force a decision. However, we all too often deny that these conflicts are internal (ours) and project them onto whatever or whomever is convenient. "Everything was OK until all this diversity stuff started." "I'd love my job if my boss weren't such a jerk." "My wife hates me so much she won't leave me." We now have either procrastination, the passing of the buck, or a fight, rather than some action better focused on the issues at hand. If, however, we would look empoweringly past our tendency to blame, worry, complain, or invoke any number of other energy sponges, we could give ourselves the opportunity to play a win/ win, infinite game with our conflicts.

The closely related organizational syndrome of crisis management too often stems from the finite perspective of time. This view sees "sooner" as being better than "later," causing the impossible stress of multiple and conflicting number-one priorities. When two priorities cannot fit within existing limitations of time and human resources, rather than focusing our attention and energy on blaming, complaining, and worrying, we could focus that energy on doing what needs to be done. In this case, a more potent use of energy would be to focus on clarifying priorities or attaining assistance. Notice that by fully focusing on doing one project to completion and then focusing on another a person will generally receive better results than by trying to juggle work on several projects. The infinite idea that time provides opportunity allows one thing to come before another without diminishing either.

Although it is easy to recommend getting help to clarify priorities or to obtain assistance, however, we are often fearful that asking for help might put us in a bad light. Then, we have trapped ourselves into a "dammed if we do and damned if we don't," no-possibility situation where ultimately everybody loses, including the organization. From the infinite perspective, having direct and open conversations about needing help would not be threatening and could move the dilemma toward a win/ win resolution of clarified priorities or additional help. Many managers bemoan episodes of employees having missed deadlines by lamenting, "Why didn't you let me know you were in trouble?"

In the case of the client not wanting a person of color as an account executive, a face-to-face meeting with the client in which the concerns are taken seriously, the cultural issues are openly identified and discussed, and the business rationale behind the new diversity policy is explained can lead to further definition of the problem along with an effective resolution. Such resolutions could include multicultural training for account executives, the placement of a more experienced person of color with the client, or the willingness to give the current account executive another opportunity.

The Impediment of Limited Self-Definition

Another impediment to focusing our intellectual energy productively is our tendency to concentrate on maintaining, protecting, and limiting our stories of who we are—our identities. As we empower ourselves, we put less and less of our energy into ego-defending activities. In the infinite game of empowerment, I do not limit who I am and how I might behave to the stories or definitions of "self" that I learned as I was growing up. I no longer limit my definition of myself to "right/not wrong," for example, not allowing myself the effectiveness of learning from different ideas and opinions that I, finitely, must define and attack as "wrong."

Of special importance is how we define ourselves regarding our intellectual ability or lack thereof. Some of us were taught that we were "dumb," "not very bright," or in some fashion "limited" in our intellectual ability. Many of us—women, in particular—were taught that we were "dumb" in mathematics. Whenever our identity or stories about ourselves include such limitations, we reenact them because we believe those stories are accurate portrayals of ourselves. Accordingly, we constrain our ability to learn. We limit our curiosity. And curiosity and learning are key aspects of our empowerment.

Part of the problem, as mentioned in the previous chapter, is that we take our stories about ourselves too seriously. When being "smart" or being "the boss" is important to my self-esteem, I must vigorously defend against any perceived attack on my intelligence or authority—whether I know what I'm talking about or not, or whether such defense is productive or not. Beware one pitfall, however: Those who surrender their positions on behalf of maintaining peace or the appearance of conformity often become angry, resentful, and unproductive. In addition, many a fine idea has been lost or never offered for fear of causing conflict and because of the need to conform. Empowered and playing infinitely, our self-esteem is not at risk, nor is conformity needed for its sense of safety. We are free to contribute fully, maintain our pride in ourselves without having to put anyone else down, and stay involved until discussion generates even better ideas that everyone can own.

At a more personal level, as I consider myself "knowledgeable" about you, I assume that you presently are the same kind of person I believed you to be in the past. In my "smartness" I pay little attention to you as you are at this moment and will miss whatever gift of yourself you may have for me at this moment. Only when I am curious can I appreciate and enjoy who you are *now* and who I am *now*. This stands in contrast to how we manage too many of our relationships. We believe in "getting to know" people from the perspective that once I "know" you, I no longer need to "get to know you." When is the last time you stopped to check what some of the important people in your life are like *now*? Do you treat your mother or father as the parents you saw them as 20, 30 years ago? How about your spouse? Checked in with him or her lately? How about your children? At work, when did you last check on your boss to see what this person is like now? How about your employees, your colleagues, or your competition? Have they not changed at all over the years? Are you the same person you were 15 years ago? So many of our relationships (including the one with ourselves) have become mediocre, indifferent, dispassionate, stagnant, and unproductive. We have assumed that we "know" these people and that there is no more to know about them—ourselves included. How deadly! How monotonous when the actuality could be quite lively, productive, exciting, and empowering. Try being curious, and watch your relationships come back to life!

To empower ourselves through our ability to learn, we must cease limiting our self-definitions to "smart" or "ignorant" as if they were mutually exclusive. Only when I allow myself to be ignorant can I become smarter. Only when I am ignorant can I be curious. Through being curious I can give myself the spaces of listening, looking, learning, and growing.

Often a deep sense of serenity and renewed energy is experienced as we focus less and less on protecting our sense of identity and self-esteem. Some fear the loss of identity in such a process. After all, who would I be without my identity? However, our stories of our "selves" won't go away—only the importance we attach to them. Empowered, we understand that our sense of identity relates only a small part of the story of who we are. Accordingly, we no longer hold our identity as important enough to defend and protect. From such a perspective, being right, and being a winner no longer hold their formerly intoxicating charm. Differences no longer are useful in defining who wins and who loses; instead, differences are appreciated and valued as opportunities for curiosity, excitement, creativity, and learning about ourselves, others, and how to make our lives at work and at home more satisfying and productive.

Empowered, we can use our intellectual energy to be curious. We can choose to appreciate those who disagree with us as people telling their stories of what they think is best, thus contributing to our stories of what works. Being curious we can freshen our relationships and aim for greater intimacy. Through the empowered use of our intellectual energy we can offer ourselves opportunity after opportunity to grow as individuals and expand our possibilities.

Linda at age 48 was comfortable in her job as a senior finance officer. Her colleagues thought well of her and her work. She was also comfortable with John, her attractive husband of 13 years. Her life was as her stories told her it should be.

Yet, in spite of her success and comfort, she felt a disquieting restlessness at times. Occasionally she would feel as if she were just managing a bunch of "bean counters," and consider turning her department inside-out into a proactive, service-oriented department. In relating this desire to John she said, "I would really love to do that kind of work—supporting people and their departments so they can truly use their budgets more wisely and productively. But I don't have the background, and no one's asking for it. Besides, I don't want to upset the apple cart; I'm basically comfortable with what I'm doing."

There are many people who, like Linda, are comfortable but not really satisfied with the status quo. To be comfortable is to feel safe. We often use the excuse of comfort to hide from ourselves the images of how we would really like our organizations, our careers, our lives to be. Such excuses, especially when coupled with our stories that bring in doubt our inherent excellence, support us in resigning ourselves to the comfort of what is in hand, known, and safe. This contrasts with the mixed emotions of excitement and fear that comes with discovering the limitless possibilities of living our lives according to our own design supported by an awareness of our own inherent excellence.

The infinite perspective allows us to play with the rules we use to guide our lives and redesign them as desired. The infinite perspective allows us to invent and create our future and our inherent excellence as we prefer them to be. Because the infinite perspective allows us to see time as opportunity, it is no longer an enemy. Contrary to the traditional rule that says, "If I'm really OK, I must to do this by myself," we can invite others to support us in navigating the unfamiliar territory of our own empower-ment. These journeys to personal or organizational empowerment are rarely successful if we embark on them as solitary travelers. Many peers, subordinates, even bosses are likely to become fellow travelers if we build or have built sound partnerships with them and if we ask them to join us or support our journey. If they choose a different journey we know that they will be OK without us, that we will be OK without them, and that we can find other companions or companies who will join and support us.

The Importance of Discovering Goals and Maintaining Focus

One of the major obstacles to living our lives the way we want is the idea that we don't know how we would like our lives to be different. We, the authors, have both spent hours with adult learners who consistently say to themselves and us, "I don't know what I want." One empowering strategy for finding out what you want can include looking back to the dream you had as a teenager or young adult. If they are not followed, such dreams stay with us as nagging sources of discontentment or as guideposts to follow toward our preferred future. Another such strategy would be to fantasize what you would love to be doing with your life if all constraints and restraints were removed.

For us to implement such strategies, though, we must choose to put aside the story that we don't know what we want. In actuality, we do know what we want, though we will often use ideas about our insufficiency, the implausibility of our desires, lack of money, family responsibilities, or any of a host of other constraints to distract us from that knowledge.

Once we discover our goals, to achieve them we must not only focus on them but also *maintain* that focus. The essential job of maintaining focus is to *regain* our focus whenever we notice that we have lost it. Some of us are naturally better at this than others, yet everyone can benefit from practice. Here is a helpful exercise that can be used in the workplace or at home to practice maintaining focus.

Maintaining Focus: An Exercise

Find a comfortable, quiet place where you won't be interrupted for at least 15 minutes. If necessary, let those around you know that you will be busy alone for a short while. Sit down or stretch out, and close your eyes. Take in a deep breath, then release it and any tensions in your body at the same time. Do this 10 or 15 times until you feel totally relaxed. Now, allow to arise in yourself an image or feeling of yourself exhibiting inherent excellence in your preferred future. This image or feeling is the part of you that is already inherently excellent. Allow yourself to simply *be* with that feeling or image.

At some point you will most likely notice that your attention has wandered to thoughts about other things, such as this is a waste of time or what you have to do tomorrow. Each time that happens, gently and without judgment bring your focus back to seeing or feeling yourself as inherently excellent in your preferred future. This refocusing is the important part of the exercise.

Do this exercise once each day, preferably twice a day. With practice you will become more and more adept at it. Again, the main purpose is to learn how to refocus your attention gently each time it wanders; this is the skill essential to maintaining focus.

Once we have chosen and focused upon our preferred future and made ourselves aware of our inherent excellence, we are ready to take the remaining steps to self-empowerment ourselves and deal with "the enemy [that] is us." Once those barriers are down, there is nothing between us and the preferred future that embodies our own inherent excellence.

Being Passionate: Emotional Empowerment

Empowered, we can focus the energy of our emotions on achieving the goals of our intellect. We call such focused emotion *passion*. Passion in this sense contrasts with the confusion of mixed or denied emotions which often seem like loose cannons when their pent-up expression explodes. Such explosions have given emotions their frightening aspect and bad name.

Empowered, we understand that our emotions are energy. We understand that we possess emotions, that emotions do not possess us. Normally, we say "I am angry" or "I am happy" as if these feelings were who we are. Hence, we act as victims of our emotions. Empowered, we use the energy of our emotions as we choose and direct. We see that emotions are like hands; they are tools we have been given, not masters for whom we must act as tools. Thus, we take charge, fully recognizing that our emotions do not own us. Renew your power over your emotions; don't allow them to master you, automatically and unthinkingly directing your behavior.

Empowered, we can be curious about our emotions, come to understand them, and use them as we wish. We've already discussed that emotion, literally defined, means "to move out" and that emotion and motivate both have the same root meaning of "to move." We understand that our emotions define the degree to which we will move or act. In essence, emotions are the experience of caring and importance. The more I care about something, the stronger is the emotion I have. The more important something is to me, the stronger the emotion and the more I will tend to empower myself and act.

It is ironic that our society so highly values achievement and productivity yet devalues emotions. High levels of achievement only occur when we feel strongly about what we want to accomplish. As we have discussed, most of us have been raised to devalue, constrain, and otherwise inhibit the emotional energies that are the underpinnings of our passion. Rather than live passionately, we live and work with our joy, love, excitement, anger, and fear bound up and constrained—an experience that is tolerable at best and chronically painful at worst. We accomplish little that we feel as satisfying or productive if we lack passion, for we disempower ourselves when we devalue emotionality. When we recreate emotions so that together they constitute a systemically necessary partner for our intellect, we empower ourselves and avail ourselves of the focused passion needed to create whatever we want most in our work and in our lives.

The Two Categories of Emotion

To empower ourselves to use our emotions rather than be used by them, we may find the following descriptions of specific emotions useful. The emotions fall into two major categories: Joy and Pain.

1.   **Joy** is the sense of well-being that we feel when we experience integrity, completeness, wholeness, and full productivity. In an ultimate sense, joy, productivity, happiness, and love help us accept and deal with any and all of life's circumstances and conditions. Joy and productivity facilitate the acknowledgement and acceptance of pain as a necessary requisite for healing—the return to joy and productivity.

2.   **Pain** is the perception of a loss of integrity, productivity, wholeness, and completeness. Betrayal and rejection, for example, are painful experiences in which we sense the loss of wholeness. To be less than fully productive is to not be truly whole or complete.

Pain is also an emotional or physical signal that alerts us to the need for healing. It is an experience of discomfort culturally interpreted as negative. Correspondingly, when people experience pain or a lack of productivity, they are often thought of as "not OK" and think of themselves as "not OK." They may refuse to acknowledge their condition, hiding it from others and sometimes even from themselves. This desire to hide pain is carried out through projection, denial, repression, or other defense-mechanisms, and hence, becomes the basis of suffering at work or at home.

Because we have such finitely negative attitudes about pain, we also tend to have trouble with the following pain-related emotions:

Fear and **Anxiety** are the sensations we feel when we detect or imagine some threat of pain (its probable or potential onset). Fear and anxiety prompt us to remove ourselves from the vicinity of the threat. Anxiety can also result from the festering of unreleased, denied pain and the accompanying fear that it may erupt again.

Anger is the desire to destroy, remove, or warn away that which is perceived as a past, present, or future cause of pain. Its purpose is vengeance or the prevention of pain's reoccurrence. We too often have strongly held stories about the "not-OKness" of anger and repress it accordingly. Unfortunately, such repression keeps us from resolving dangerous situations that will cause us more pain at some later date.

Guilt is the pain that results from the perception that we caused pain. Guilt is self-blame. It commonly is derived from the socially conditioned but erroneous belief that one can cause pain in another and that causing pain makes one a bad or "not OK" person. We can cause someone else physical pain; however, emotional pain, like all emotions, is a reaction to an internal interpretation which is only in the control of the person experiencing the emotion. We will explore this notion more fully in the Chapter 9 when we describe how the mind works.

Guilt can also be the pain of our own sense of failure and worthlessness when we believe we should have done better. Punishment in some form (for example, scapegoat-hood) may be used as a means of expiation.

Sadness and **Grief** are reactions to the perception that we have lost something important to our sense of productivity, integrity, and wellbeing. Sadness often prompts us to regain what we have lost. When sadness includes the thought that the loss is permanent, grief is experienced. Grief may lead us to seek reintegration of self to regain the sense of wholeness and productivity. Depression and despair occur when we believe that wholeness and productivity cannot be regained.

Suffering is the maintenance of pain while healing is still incomplete. Sometimes it is used to avoid the acute, sharper experience of pain or for the punishment required by guilt.

Emotions range in strength from mild and unnoticeable to forceful and overwhelming. Their duration also varies. The pique of being caught by a red traffic signal, for instance, is usually so brief and minor an emotion that it goes unnoticed. Ironically, whereas we commonly express our emotions when the object of our feelings has slight or moderate value to us, we often suppress our emotions about the important elements in our lives, sometimes even denying that we have such feelings. These repressed emotions build up to the point where finally we must release them, usually doing so in an overwhelming, uncontrolled, messy fashion. As we learn to experience, focus, and express our emotions as they normally occur, we will no longer experience the overreactions that come from the sudden release of pent-up, unfinished emotional business.

Many people believe that emotional behavior will be uncontrollable if feelings are allowed full expression. This need not be so. Again, if we allow ourselves to experience our feelings as they arise, we can choose the focus and manner of their expression. We can choose to express emotion quietly or vehemently, punitively or productively. The key to such control of our emotional expression is in being conscious of our feelings. As we suppress or deny them, we surrender our conscious ability to manage their expression. Emotions *will* express themselves—if not directly, through our recognition and control of them, then indirectly, through physical or mental illness and inappropriate behavior that makes our lives and our loves more difficult than they need be.

All in all, emotions are neither good nor bad. They are crucial and necessary if we are to act on behalf of healing ourselves and creating satisfaction and productivity. The energy of emotions can be directed toward, and focused on, creativity, problem solving, and the construction and maintenance of effective relationships, rather than used debilitatingly and punitively to damage our self-esteem, our bodies, and our relationships. As we attempt to suppress, deny and, in effect, hold on to our emotions, we experience suffering and loss of productivity; but as we experience our emotions and focus them, we move closer toward achieving our goals of productivity and satisfaction—within ourselves and with others.

Empowered, we do not waste energy judging and constraining how we feel; we can express our emotions as freely or privately as we wish and use them strategically as fits our purposes and goals. If we so choose, we can use our anger and fear to galvanize ourselves into positive action rather than to fight or hide. We can use our pain as a signal to attend to the wounds and consequent loss of productivity that need our compassionate attention. This is far better than using pain to buttress blame, worry, or suffering. We can use our joy to celebrate ourselves and others, which supports even greater productivity. With our emotions focused and our passions liberated, not much will stand in our way.

Acting: Physical Empowerment

When we are intellectually empowered, having focused our minds, and emotionally empowered, having focused our emotions into passion, then we will act powerfully. This equation for the most part is a natural consequence about which not much more needs saying. However, there is one major pitfall—giving up—that needs exploration.

Ed Reese and Samuel Savonard had been friends since childhood. They were neighbors, and they both worked for the same company as account executives selling high-end furniture to corporations. Their regional sales manager announced that he was going to retire in six months and that he would choose as his replacement the account executive who produced the most over his or her quota during that six-month period. Though several of the account executives thought this was an odd way to select a successor, that was the way it was. Both Ed and Samuel set out to win the promotion.

Both encountered problems along the way. Ed became ill with a bad case of the flu which left him feeling drained for weeks, while his daughter returned home distraught from having left her husband. Samuel strained his back cleaning out his garage, and his son ran away from home. To top all that off, a recession began which was difficult for everyone.

In response to these problems, Ed began to complain to the sales manager that his method of picking a successor wasn't fair and that managerial ability should be considered. He went on to suggest that the contest be postponed until after the recession had ended and he had a chance to get well and resolve his at-home problems. The manager suggested that Ed stop complaining and focus his energy on his sales. At that, Ed began to complain to others about the sales manager's insensitivity toward his situation, said that there was no way he could win, and gave up. Samuel persisted and won the promotion.

Both Samuel and Ed were focused and passionate at the start of sales contest. But Samuel never wavered in his focus or passion, whereas Ed gave up, having lost his focus in the face of adversity. His emotions, then, powered his blaming and complaining—rationalizations of why he couldn't possibly win. He victimized himself to vindicate himself from the possibility of being a loser—quite a different focus from selling.

What Samuel had that Ed didn't have was patience and persistence. These are critical to success, particularly in the face of adversity, because they help us keep our focus and our emotions aligned with our focus. Often, patient and persistent people will achieve their goals, whereas others won't simply because they gave up. Ironically, a primary reason behind our giving up is that we have seduced ourselves with our fear of losing. Thus, our focus turns to rationalizing why we are going to lose.

Empowered intellectually and emotionally, we use our physical abilities fully, patiently, and persistently on behalf of our preferred focus. Toward this end we will also maintain our bodies, keeping them fit and in good health through effective exercise, proper eating habits, and minimal indulgence in those things that are not physically good for us. Fully empowered we enjoy our bodies for our bodies' sake. We enjoy our bodies in action playing tennis, running, working, or making love. We use our senses fully. We appreciate what we see, hear, touch, smell, and taste for the joy and wonder that our physical senses can offer us. As we use our bodies and their senses fully, they fully support us in health and well-being.

Empowered intellectually, emotionally, and physically, we are fully aware of the inherent excellence that is ours. So empowered, we work, play, and live 100 percent. Have you ever seen a two-year-old going after what he or she wants? We often speak of children in this age group as being in their "terrible twos." When they spy something they want or want to investigate, they go for it 100 percent—heart, mind, and body. However intractable they may be, perhaps they have something to teach us.

To get in touch with your ability to play 100 percent, imagine a time when you really wanted something, fully applied yourself, and got what you wanted. All of us at any number of points in our lives have had these experiences when we were clearly focused, highly passionate, and fully in action toward our goal. Make a point of remembering these times, write them down, recollect how you felt then, and play those scenes through in your mind at least once a day. When we play 100 percent, we feel good about ourselves even during those few times when we fail to reach our goal. Notice that when you played less than 100 percent, you usually got a result of less than 100 percent or felt less than 100 percent fulfilled even if you achieved your goal. Whether or not to play 100 percent is our choice. Go for it!

BUILDING EFFECTIVE INFLUENCE

Now that we are empowered as individuals, having mastered the control of our individual energies, we can leverage that energy to make us impact our world vastly beyond the scope of our individual capacities. We do this through soliciting the energies of others for use on our behalf. This is the world of influence.

It is in this arena where the dysfunctional nature of the finite perspective is most evident. Playing finitely we frequently compete against potential partners or allies and attempt to win at their expense. Yet any victory we manage to pull off is never complete, for the losers that finite winners create rarely lend their energy with any alacrity to the winners' purposes. At best, those who see themselves as losers are sullen and apathetic helpers; they lend less energy than is useful to the winners' tasks while awaiting an opportunity to escape altogether. At worst, losers can also become resentful saboteurs or angry enemies dedicated to the winners' demise. Creating losers who feel beaten or victimized is not an effective strategy for leveraging your individual power. Do you have any such relations in your life? These would include not only relationships in which you feel trapped or want revenge, but also relationships in which someone might be feeling loser to your winner. We strongly suggest that in checking this out you don't rely on your own perceptions. They often only tell us what we want to believe. Check it out directly with the particular people in question.

Using the Seven Channels to Build Partnerships

In Chapter 4 we saw how the seven channels of influence are often used as sources for power struggles. For the purposes of empowerment, we must use them to build partnerships in which all involved feel that they are getting as much as they are giving. We can do this as we recognize and free ourselves from our stories and judgments about the rightness and wrongness of the seven channels of influence. Then, all the channels become available for our use as tools to build powerful partnerships.

Nellie Friar, a relatively new department director in a medium-sized investment bank, hired a young, hard-working Wharton graduate, Jim Thomas, to run her small accounts section. Within six months nearly half of Jim's staff had quietly complained to Nellie about his overbearing, know-it-all demeanor. During that time Nellie had two conversations with Jim. In the first she avuncularly suggested that he listen closely to his very competent staff to shorten his learning curve a bit. In the second, she rather curtly pointed out that the morale of his staff could stand some improvement and that he should try harder to become more of a team member. In both meetings Jim seemed bent on thanking Nellie for having given him such a wonderful opportunity and on explaining how he was doing everything under his power to live up to the high standards of productivity set by the company.

Nellie decided to try again. During the third conversation, she said with some exasperation, "As director of this division, I insist that you pay more effective attention to the morale of your staff. It's beginning to infect other units." Smiling in his usual happy way, Jim replied, "I'll do whatever you ask; I'm just so thrilled about . . ." At which point Nellie said very quietly, "You won't be so thrilled with this letter of reprimand I've got here. This is the third time we've talked about this, and I just can't seem to get you to take this seriously. If the problem continues, you will lose the job that you're so thrilled about having." Jim, looking as if he had been struck by a thunderbolt, responded, "What third time? This is the first time I've known that something this serious was happening. Why didn't you let me know before that you were so serious?"

Jim's manager tried three distinct channels of influence before she hit upon one that worked. She offered the expertise of his staff, followed by group solidarity and position. Finally, she got his attention through the channel of coercion. Many managers decry the use of coercion, claiming that it creates an atmosphere of fear that will cause further performance deterioration as well as stimulate a generally negative environment. However, effective influence depends upon which channel will yield results from the perspective of the person to be influenced. Nellie may not have wanted to coerce Jim, yet it was the way that she finally got his attention. Jim may also have responded to the channels of attraction or reward. She might have gotten his attention by letting him know how much she admired his work ethic or by offering him the possibility of a bonus for straightening out his staff's morale problems. Regardless of which channels she preferred, if she had not been able to influence Jim, her success would have been compromised as well.

How can we find out which channel will work with another person? Asking can be useful. If the person is not familiar with the channels of influence as we've explored them, describing each until you get a positive response can produce good results. Trial by error, as Jim did above, is a surer method.

Several of our students, having learned of the channels of influence, thought that using them consciously and intentionally would be manipulative and exploitative. The channels can be used deviously and finitely. However, in doing so, we risk anger, resentment, or apathy, which would severely limit our influence. Used infinitely, with positive regard for the persons you wish to influence, more permanent and productive relationships become available to us.

As we deepen our understanding of how infinitely related our personal, organizational, and world systems are, we better understand that our survival, productivity, and satisfaction are dependent upon the survival, productivity, and satisfaction of our partners in our planet-wide community. Accordingly, we will use our personal energies to build infinite partnerships rather than continue strategies of discrimination, conflict, and war.

Empowered Equity

Equity is the arena in which we can maintain and further build the effectiveness of our partnerships. All of us try to ensure that we get a fair return on the energy we use on someone else's behalf. With little return, we experience dissatisfaction and will accordingly lower the amount of energy we use on someone else's behalf. With a greater return, we experience higher equity, greater satisfaction, and the willingness to continue or increase our use of energy on someone else's behalf.

Playing infinitely calls for us to ensure that all players experience a high level of equity and satisfaction in return for their playing the game with us. This translates into me using my energy on behalf of your goals as well as you using your energy on behalf of my goals. This is the essence of partnership and playing the infinite game of power. If my partners are looking out for my equity and I am looking out for theirs, our mutual gain and satisfaction are guaranteed—a game of mutually high equity that can continue forever. Moreover, the sense of having been of service to others is, in and of itself, a major source of equity and satisfaction for both me and my partners. And if I must refuse to provide service because the demands or requests would put my sense of equity too far out of sync, I will expend little energy on guilt and self-recrimination.

A major pitfall to avoid is our tendency to respond to a drop in our equity with attempts to lower the other person's equity, when a more rational response would be to attempt to restore our own. If, for example, my equity has slipped, I may notice a vague, ill-defined sense of dissatisfaction. Not being clear, I don't say anything about it; however, I find myself either dragging my feet or arguing about things that used to be inconsequential. What I am doing is lowering the other person's degree of influence with me. I am saying, "If my returns have decreased, yours must decrease too." If we cannot have high equity, we choose to reestablish equity by lowering the equity of others. Now, I've begun a series of finite games. Dissatisfied, the other person is likely to allow me less influence with him or her. Game two goes to me. If this pattern persists, we will lower each other's equity until the equity gets so low that one of us withdraws from the relationship altogether. If I'm your manager, I fire you or you find another job. If we're friends, we stop seeing each other. If married, we separate or divorce.

The Five Steps to Rebuilding Mutual High Equity

If my equity is low and I want to play infinitely, my goal is to continue our relationship and find some way to influence you so that you can help me get my equity back up without lowering yours. Too often, however, I don't notice that I'm not playing infinitely until I notice that the relationship is in danger. To help you rebuild to mutual high equity, we offer the following steps:

1. **Make your primary goal rebuilding the relationship to mutual high equity**. This first step is critically important. Without it, we tend to focus our efforts on getting what we want from the other person, which is a waste of energy as the other person has low equity as well and is wary of our influence. This usually leads to more finite behavior on both sides, regardless of the best of intentions.

2. **Check out your assumptions about the other person**. We usually attempt to figure out why the other person is not treating us as well as we would like. As a result we develop certain assumptions that we come to hold firmly as truth. For example, "My skill threatens him"; "She thinks I want her job"; "He never really liked me in the first place"; "He's a golden-haired boy now"; "He's angry with me because I . . . "; "She's a control freak, and I won't let her control me." Occasionally, our assumptions are accurate, and we use those instances to reinforce our belief in our assumptions. More often they become self-fulfilling prophecies; we treat someone as if the assumption were true, get a negative reaction, and then say, "I told you so."

It is more effective to ask the person whether or not our assumptions are true, or at least give him or her the benefit of the doubt, understanding that our assumptions are not necessarily accurate and may misinterpret the other person's goals, motivation, or feelings. Frequently, conversations that start out checking assumptions have a very positive impact on equity as we "clear the air" and revise our assumptions.

3. Seek to increase the other person's equity before increasing yours. This is a paraphrase of "Seek first to understand, then to be understood," from Stephen Covey's *The Seven Habits of Highly Effective People* (1990, p. 237). As the other person's equity becomes high again, he or she is increasingly willing to use energy on your behalf again. It may be difficult to remember to take this step, but doing so is essential to rebuilding satisfying, effective, and productive relationships. Being curious about, interested in, and appreciative of the other person's feelings, assumptions, and goals are enormously useful here.

4. Get clear about what you want and ask for it. Getting clear about what you want takes some time and thought. You may want to recruit a friend to help you with this step. Once clear about what you want, notice all the reasons you have for not asking others for it. These could include being ridiculed, being obligated, being seen as needy, or otherwise being made vulnerable. Next notice the risks of not asking. In that list, not getting what you want will certainly appear, as well as the risk of losing a desirable relationship. Most of the time, the risks of *not* asking outweigh the risks of asking. Most of our fears of asking are self-coercive and derive from past experiences that don't apply to our current situations.

5. Discuss and negotiate, discuss and negotiate. Conversation involving the four prior steps must continue until you reach a resolution that will lead to high equity for both parties. Patience is needed to straighten out misunderstandings and to deal with hard-to-handle emotions. Passion is needed to convey how important the negotiations are to you, how much you care about the other party and your relationship, and how vital your interests are to achieving your goals. Persistence is needed when your patience seems about to run out, when the discussion needs several days to conclude, or when the other person is willing to let you win and thus accept a loss.

There are two possible win/win conclusions to the discussions. The most preferred is a win/win that includes the continuation of the relationship. The other is a win/win that includes ending the relationship. The latter can be problematic, though not necessarily. There are situations in which we have arguably concluded that ending the relationship will be best for both parties. This could be my quitting, my firing you, my ending our friendship. You may not agree that ending the relationship is in my best interests or yours. Your best judgment, that assessment which you fully judge to be trustworthy after double-checking and reality-testing three or four times—is what you have to go by. If these steps have been followed with integrity, you may discover that the dismissed person will renew contact later on and thank you. Michael, during a two-year stint as director of Human Resources at a major-market network television station, had this experience several times.

The next time you're feeling dissatisfied with life, *focus on something you care about and get yourself in motion.* Certainly, an over-simplification of this chapter, but still a useful and pungent statement to hold on to. All you need now is to believe in yourself. That's what the next chapter is about.

CHAPTER NINE:

SELF-DISCOVERING YOUR INHERENT EXCELLENCE

Discovering and acting upon our inherent excellence may be the most difficult task in our journey toward living empowering lives. At first glance it seems the easiest, because most of us have been taught to maintain at least a veneer of "I'm OK" in the face of almost any insult or circumstance. Yet not far beneath this veneer lie the self-deprecating, self-defeating, self-demolishing stories and beliefs about ourselves that we all too often use to direct our emotions and actions.

Our veneer of "I'm OK" is at best a poor relation to our fundamental inherent excellence, which at its base is our *knowledge of our ability to create our own experience from moment to moment.* Many of us decry how dreary or depressed we feel on cloudy, drizzly days as if the weather was in charge of how we feel. We say, "You make me so angry!" or " That makes me so sad!" or "They make me so happy!" as if we had no choice in the matter.

TWO METHODS OF EXPERIENCING INHERENT EXCELLENCE

We offer you two processes for experiencing your inherent excellence. They involve owning your shadow and owning responsibility for your thoughts, feelings, and actions.

Owning Your Shadow

The biggest barrier to empowering ourselves and experiencing our inherent excellence is the set of limitations created by our stories about who we are and, more importantly, who we are not. We use the Jungian term *shadow* for the *who-we-are-not* portion of ourselves. Locked in our shadow is a great deal of our energy. Ironically, we use even more energy to keep the energy in our shadows locked up. Before we can release that energy, we need to see that doing so is safe and useful. To begin that process, try the following exercise. You'll need a sheet of paper and a pen or pencil.

Shadow Exercise

First, list nine words that describe who you are. They can be adjectives, nouns, or verbs; it doesn't matter.

```
Smart
Energetic
Loving
Successful
Male
Fun-loving
Helpful
Open
Easygoing
```

Next, think about each word; put an "X" in front of it if that characteristic is essential to who you are. For instance, if we (the authors) were not *smart* we just wouldn't be ourselves. We would still be ourselves, however, if we were not *energetic*. Got it?

```
X  Smart
   Energetic
   Loving
   Successful
X  Male
   Fun-loving
X  Helpful
   Open
X  Easygoing
```

The "Xs" mark the self-definitions on which you probably focus most of your energy, verifying, protecting, and defending them whenever you feel challenged. It is likely that if you act in ways that run counter to these definitions, or if others think you have acted in such ways, you will expend much energy feeling upset, angry, insulted, hurt, afraid, ashamed, or humiliated. Is this true for you? Would you like to use that energy in more empowering ways? If so, we'll get to that.

Next, in a column to the right, list those words that represent *your* psychological opposites for the first list. Do not be concerned with dictionary-accurate opposites; record whatever feels like the opposite to you.

X	Smart	Stupid
	Energetic	Lazy
	Loving	Uncaring
	Successful	Failure
X	Male	Female
	Fun-loving	Dull
X	Helpful	Insensitive
	Open	Closed
X	Easygoing	Caring

This second list of words represents the characteristics that seem to be "not you," that don't fit your story about yourself. They are parts of your shadow. Have you ever in some way felt or acted in the ways described by the words on this second list? Have you put much energy into not doing so? Have you ever wanted to act that way? What feelings do you experience as you review that list? Look closely at your feelings. Notice whether you feel at all uncomfortable or anxious. Such feelings are a clear tip-off that these are characteristics of your shadow. It's OK if you feel this way; you are getting closer to making that energy available to yourself.

Do a third column. In this column we are going to reframe the negative words of the second column. Think up words or short phrases that essentially mean the same *to you* as the negative words in the second column, but that are positive or neutral in connotation. Look at our list to see what we mean. If your second column word is positive and your first column word is negative, reframe the negative word in the first column. If you consider neither word negative, skip that pair. You may find this more difficult than the first two lists and need some help. Consult a thesaurus or dictionary, or ask someone else for ideas. Reject any ideas that *in your view* do not essentially correspond to the meaning of the term you're dealing with; likewise, reject ideas that do not have positive or neutral connotations *to you*.

X	Smart	Stupid	Ignorant
	Energetic	Lazy	Resting
	Loving	Uncaring	Being private
	Successful	Failure	Something to learn from
X	Male	Female	Nurturing
	Fun-loving	Dull	Serious
X	Helpful	Insensitive	Inward focused
	Open	Closed	Introvertive
X	Easygoing	Intense	Passionate

Notice that how you feel about a word depends on the way you look at it. Given the positive or neutral "reframing," you may be finding it easier to accept those "negative" parts of yourself from the second list.

Also notice how the reframed word (third list) is a characteristic that can, in some way, actually help you achieve the corresponding characteristic in your first list and support you in being more receptive to the characteristic in your second list. Through being *ignorant* (third list) we have the opportunity to become even *smarter*. Through *resting* we can regain our energy to be *energetic* again. Through *being private* we can give ourselves the personal time we need, so we won't resent giving time to those we love. Through learning from our *failures* we can create even more *success*. Through being *passionate* we can be influential when being *easygoing* isn't enough.

How did it work for you? Can you see some of the "shadow parts" of yourself more clearly now? Can you also see how those shadow parts are not only OK, but very useful?

Other Tools for Owning Your Shadow

There are many other useful ways for owning our shadows, even if it is a never-ending task. The poet Robert Bly has written a wonderful little book titled *The Little Book on the Human Shadow*. We found it very useful for "eating our shadow," as he calls the process of owning your shadow. He offers some very simple techniques for writing poetry in such a way that you will reveal your shadow to yourself. A side benefit is that you will discover your poetic side without having to deal with any rules about the way poetry should be written.

There are also many workshops and books that are useful to the shadow-owning process. In the appendix are lists of workshops and books that we have experienced and read and personally found useful. Whatever shadow-owning process you use, be prepared to practice, to be disciplined about your practice, and to succeed.

Owning our shadow is a way for us to experience the wholeness, the completeness of ourselves that includes inherent excellence. For most of us, our experience of our inherent excellence is buried fairly deeply in our unconscious under the morass of self-doubts and self-deceptions associated with characteristics of our shadow. As we bring the shadow to consciousness, make peace with our self-doubts, and clear-up our self-deceptions, the experience of our inherent excellence can also become conscious. In the process, we also unleash for our conscious and purposeful use the energy that constitutes our not-me parts. We regain as well the energy that we have used to keep those parts of us inaccessible.

Owning Responsibility for Your Thoughts, Emotions, and Actions

Responsibility is a word that brings with it mixed emotions and mixed blessings. On one hand, we *should* be "responsible" and accept "responsibility." "Responsible" is the right way to be. On the other hand, many power struggles are about "who is responsible" with each side claiming, "Not me!" Our early training clearly suggests that we are not responsible for our own feelings, although we may be responsible for the feelings of others. We assert that another person can make us happy or angry. "You make me so angry!" or "You would make me so happy if . . ." are good examples. As children we often heard such statements and learned them well. The idea behind these statements is that feelings are caused by external circumstances and are not our responsibility.

So used, *responsibility* generally implies fault or blame for something gone wrong or that might go wrong. To be responsible too often implies the possibility of being wrong, and to be wrong rather than right is clearly to be a loser rather than a winner. Of course, being responsible for something that has gone well or that is likely to go well is linked with taking credit, and thus is highly acceptable. Power struggles ensue when someone else thinks he or she deserves "the credit," as if credit, like power, were finite. Given this win/lose dynamic, there is often high risk and a sense of burden involved in being responsible. We usually consider this risk and burden as best avoided even though being responsible is a "good" way to be.

As an issue of power, however, to have no responsibility is also to give ourselves no choice about what we think, feel, or do. And to be without choice in such matters is to victimize ourselves while blaming others or external circumstances, acting as though we have little or no power or influence over our own lives or portions thereof. As we recognize, rethink, and assume responsibility for our experience and our behavior, we rediscover our power and ability to act in the world as befits our inherent excellence.

Stephan used to be chronically bored with his life. His boredom was occasionally broken by fits of rage and bouts of depression. For years he blamed others for his situation. His mother was to blame because she had discouraged him from going to medical school saying it would be "such hard work." His father was to blame because he had been such a wimpy role model. His wife was to blame because of her consistently patronizing and demeaning statements, such as "You sure are a fine little fixer!" and "If you were as brainy as you are strong, you sure wouldn't need me!"

That's how he used to be. With the support of our Power Lab and the new friends he made there, he realized that his boredom was rooted in the belief that he was not aggressive enough and not very bright and that this belief was founded on no more than "old stories." These stories were taught to him with all good intention by his parents and unwittingly reinforced by his wife. As he had this insight, he also noticed stories from his teachers, most of whom would compliment him on how bright he was and support their compliments with top grades. From these insights, Stephan decided to write his own script about how he felt about himself, how he wanted his life to be, and about his abilities to create that life for himself.

Today, Stephen is a licensed C.P.A. with an M.B.A. and works for a consulting firm. His wife notices that he still gets perturbed when his parents try to warn him about the dangers of setting up his own business, but he does not allow such feelings to get in his way anymore. His wife is having a difficult time with his changes but is genuinely working at seeing him as brainy as well as strong, with a mind of his own. In assuming responsibility for his own feelings, Stephan is turning his life around and entering the arena of infinite power.

Then there is Kelley's story:

Kelley, like many people, would feel wonderful and at peace as she watched a gorgeous sunset or when she was relaxing on vacation at the ocean with the sun beaming down on her. On one vacation, she went scuba diving for the first time. Moving weightlessly among the coral and the many-hued fish, she experienced a sense of peace, wonder, and oneness even stronger than she did with her sunsets. She saw some other divers much deeper than she and knew they were having the same experience. She felt as one with them as with everything around her.

She returned home reflecting on her experience and vowing to become a licensed scuba diver. During an evening of such reflection, she began to wonder if she could have that experience without having to dive. At some point in her reveries, she startled herself by noticing that she was then having that experience of peace and oneness—just as intense, just as peaceful.

Kelley decided that her experience of peace was not contingent on sunsets or beaches or scuba diving or other special circumstances. She decided that her experiences were her own and with her always. She calls upon them whenever she relaxes and focuses her attention upon feeling wonderful, peaceful, and at one with the world. She recognizes that the way she stops herself is through taking too seriously her old stories—the stories that say that her experiences of joy or pain are contingent on external events or other people.

Kelley may still get upset over certain incidents in her life and argue with people, such as her boss, but she has chosen to accept the responsibility for how strongly those incidents and arguments affect the quality of her life and her experience of the world. In doing so, she has altered her perception of power, moving from the finite to the infinite perspective. Because she now sees upsetting incidents as just events in the continuing infinite game she is playing, she is more apt to control them, rather than let them control her. Assuming this responsibility for one's own feelings, the quality of one's experiences, and one's self-perception has been Kelley's *choice*—and it can be our choice. Ironically, even if we choose to see others as responsible for our feelings, we are still choosing—just unconsciously. Since you choose either way, you may as well choose the option that works best for you!

Accepting responsibility is easier and more powerful if we reframe our definition of it as "our ability to choose our own responses." From this definition, responsibility only exists in the present. We have no choice about the past; we've already made those choices for better or worse. We cannot make choices in the future because the future, when it seems to have arrived, has become the present. Hence, our ability to choose only exists right now. The sense of burden, fault, blame, and win/lose risk is removed with this definition and is replaced with a sense of opportunity and power.

The Seven Steps of How the Mind Works

Let's take an empowering look at how our minds work so that we can better understand the reality of our having choices about how we think, feel, and behave. There are seven steps involved in how our minds receive a particular piece of data, decide what it means, and react accordingly. The following chart lays out these steps and provides a disempowering and an empowering example.

The Steps	Disempowered Manager	Empowered Manager
1. Event occurs.	Employee turns page of newspaper.	Employee turns page of newspaper.
2. Sensation is received.	Manager sees leftward motion of object in hand.	Manager sees leftward motion of object in hand.
3. Interpretation of "what"	Employee is reading sports section.	Employee is reading newspaper.
4. Interpretation of "why"	Employee is goofing off and blatantly challenging authority of manager.	Employee may be checking something related to his or her work.
5. Makes judgement re: safe/not safe	Not safe: Self-esteem is at stake.	Safe: Self-esteem is not at stake.
6. Emotional reaction	Anxiety and anger	Curiosity
7. Behavior to maintain or protect self-esteem	Sarcastically asks if employee has already finished all his or her work.	Asks employee what he or she is reading about.

Event Occurs. This is the factual event that occurred in the external world. As in our example, the actual amount of data used by our minds is often very small. In our example, "Employee turns page of newspaper." (This is actually an interpretation, as we will see in the next two steps, but is used here for purposes of clarity.)

Sensation Received. This describes the sensory mechanism by which our physical selves receive information of the event. This involves a screening process. Our sensory mechanisms allow relatively small amounts of data into our systems.

Interpretation of "what." This is the step in which the mind takes over. It assigns meaning to the data received. First, it determines what the event is; second, it interprets the purpose of the event (why it's happening—Step four). In our example, "Employee is reading newspaper" is the "what" interpretation offered under Empowered.

The process of interpretation is analogous to that of finding a specific part of a movie that you have on a videotape. You have in your mind an image of the part you are trying to find. You scan through the tape until you find a scene on the tape similar to the image in your mind. Accordingly, the managers scan through the "tapes" in their minds looking for an image similar to "leftward motion of object in hand." Of course, our minds provide much greater detail and complexity than our simple example, as well as much greater speed than a VCR. The manager finds such an image from his own experience of reading the sports section at work, and thus assigns the same basic meaning to the new data. His "knowledge" is more detailed than that of the empowered manager, who also has applied an image from his own experience in order to determine what the data means.

The "tapes" in our minds are records of our past experiences. They include knowledge gained from personal experience, such as that tasting an apple is enjoyable or that feeling an electric shock is painful. Also included is second hand knowledge, such as the moon is a sphere, which is gained from accepting the word of someone else, for example, a teacher or an author. These tapes cover our entire life's history. Their sum equals our beliefs about reality—about ourselves, others, and the world. Most of us tend to hold these beliefs as unquestionable and inviolable reality.

We now have our first difference between the disempowered and empowered perspectives. The manager with the disempowered perspective has no doubt about what was seen—"Employee is reading sports section," even though he has no sensory data this specific. His story is based on what section of the paper he would have been reading had he been caught in such a situation. That's what his mind came up with and that is what he believes is so. The empowered perspective, however, knows that his mind's interpretations of what are often untrustworthy and does not over-specify, hence, "Employee is reading newspaper." It leaves room for new information since the present may not be like the past, regardless of how many times a particular interpretation may have been accurate. Persistent openness to the possibility of new information or new ideas is a critical aspect of empowerment. As important, the empowered person *consciously chooses* an interpretation of what is going on.

Interpretation of "why." A second level of interpretation occurs to give meaning to the first level of interpretation. This level often answers the question "Why?" "Employee is reading sports section" because "Employee is goofing off and blatantly challenging the authority of the manager." He clearly remembered reading a newspaper at his desk because he knew it would upset his boss. Again, notice the assumption that what was so in his past is applicable to the present situation. Even if the interpretation is not a negative one, for example, the employee is (not "may be") checking something related to his or her work, it still may not be accurate. In either case, assuming an interpretation is accurate is potentially disempowering. Assumptions close off the possibility of new data and new ideas, hence, learning and creativity. They also leave a lot of room for power struggles about who's "right" if the assumptions are ever challenged. Again, persistent openness to the possibility of new information or new ideas is critical to empowerment, learning, creativity, and the avoidance of power struggles over who is right. The empowered person consciously chooses interpretations of "why" or "what" that leave room for something different.

Makes judgment re safe/not safe. Once we have completed our interpretations, we will judge whether or not this situation is safe or dangerous to our physical or psychological selves. This step is key as it provides initial guidance for what we should do about an event as sensed and interpreted.

We base these judgments, too, upon the stories and rules developed from our past experience and from second hand knowledge, such as community teachings. Our disempowered manager has automatically judged the situation of the employee reading a newspaper as not safe. His self-esteem is endangered because he has finite rules that say (1) he should be a good manager, and (2) good managers do not have employees who goof off. This manager also has another set of rules that say (1) employees who goof off are challenging the authority of their managers, and (2) it is not OK to have managerial authority challenged. His self-esteem is doubly and intolerably endangered, or so his stories tell him. Notice how this manager has placed his self-esteem in the hands of his employees.

The empowered manager has rules as well. However, his rules are of the infinite variety. One of his rules is "Don't make assumptions about other people's motivations without sufficient data." Another is "Base your self-esteem on your own judgments, not that of others." Given these rules, this manager feels quite safe. The empowered person, through consciously choosing an interpretation, also chooses the feelings or emotions he or she will have.

It is useful to note that intellectual energy is the basis for steps one through five. The mind is so efficient that all this mental activity takes place within moments. The bulk of this activity is also unconscious and unnoticeable, particularly for the disempowered persons who are not aware of their stories or rules. Empowered persons may have noticed some stories and rules similar to that of the disempowered manager. Through being conscious of them, however, they are able to refocus their attention and thoughts on the infinite.

Emotional reaction. At this point, emotional energy comes into play. The disempowered manager has feelings of anxiety and anger. When we have feelings of anxiety we are feeling threatened, to which there are two primary emotional responses—fear and anger. Both can occur together and are instinctual emotional reflexes to situations of danger. In situations of physical danger, the reflexive nature of these emotional reactions can be lifesaving. When the danger is not life-threatening, as with self-esteem issues, the reactions of fear and anger too often lead us to unnecessary power struggles. We are trying to protect something that we can only protect within ourselves.

The empowered manager, given his infinite rules about maintaining the game (the games of teaching and learning in this case) and keeping his sense of self-esteem within his own control, feels curious—curious about why the employee is reading a newspaper and whether or not it is relevant to work.

Behavior to maintain or protect self-esteem. This is where we go into physical action. If the emotional reactions are strong enough, our bodies prepare for action with increases in our heart rate, breathing, and flow of adrenalin. In the case of sufficient threat, we will choose flight (fear is stronger than anger) or fight (anger is stronger than fear). Our disempowered manager is angry. He has another rule, however, which says that vehement expressions of anger are not OK. So, he resorts to thinly veiled sarcasms attempting to use the influence channels of expertise and coercion. In a voice loud enough to awaken the dead, he shouts, "It's OK to read the newspaper in my department if you've already finished all your work for the day! Have you, Mr. Jones?" The manager, feeling wronged and threatened, has also attempted to regain his equity by giving as good, if not better, than he thinks he has gotten—in this case, humiliation.

Feeling no sense of threat from his interpretations, the empowered manager motivates himself with curiosity. He approaches the employee and quietly asks, "What are you reading? Anything interesting?" He has based his self-esteem as a manager on improving his ability to build and maintain the infinite equity of the manager/employee relationship. And he has kept to himself the right to approve or disapprove of his efforts. Moreover, even if the empowered manager chooses an interpretation that triggers a reaction of anger, because he is aware of his stories he can still choose to act as described from the infinite perspective. He might at some later time sort out for himself what story or tape he had played to trigger the anger.

In either the empowered or the disempowered case, the manager's action would be a new event for the employee, who would go through the same seven steps in response. The employee's response would be a new event for the manager, who would again go through the seven steps, which would be another new event for the employee, ad infinitum.

We can use our minds on automatic and, given the rules and stories that we have grown up with, play the games of life finitely with their attendant power struggles and dubious satisfactions. Or, we can do the work of discovering our inherent excellence through owning our shadows and owning responsibility for our thoughts, feelings, and actions. With *knowledge of our ability to create our own experience from moment to moment* we can empower ourselves to play the games of life infinitely for joy and productivity.

CHAPTER TEN:

MAKING SELF-EMPOWERMENT WORK

We have explored the three principle actions of empowerment (focusing, being passionate, and acting), two methods for discovering our inherent excellence, and some pitfalls we must avoid on the way to the experience of empowerment. Now we will explore four additional behaviors that empowered people use in day-to-day living to combat those pitfalls, exercise their empowerment, and support their experience of inherent excellence. They include being curious, speaking powerfully, developing a support system, and being patient with ourselves.

THE FOUR WAYS TO MAKE SELF-EMPOWERMENT WORK

Being Curious

Being curious is a particularly useful means of empowerment. Curiosity is the desire for new knowledge or information. When confronted by that which is unfamiliar or different, curiosity can point us in the direction of learning and personal growth. As curiosity is often a prerequisite for learning, supposedly it is a prized virtue because we value learning. In actual practice, however, we seem to have difficulty maintaining our sense of curiosity in the face of our finite tendencies regarding power.

The usual trigger for curiosity is an awareness of something with which we are unfamiliar. We can use our curiosity, then, to explore that unfamiliarity until it becomes known—a usable definition of learning. We also can extend this usefulness to any idea, attitude, belief, or behavior that is different from our own. This extension of curiosity's applicability, however, runs contrary to our normal and finite reactions. In our traditional finite world, differences are not safe. They are dangerous because they are the basis for establishing who will be winner and who will be loser. Consequently, we feel most comfortable with those who are most like us and things and ideas with which we are familiar. Yet although such a world may indeed feel safe and comfortable, it offers us little or no opportunity for curiosity and the learning, growth, and the exploration of our inherent excellence that we can gain from that which is different or unfamiliar.

If we are willing to be curious about that which is different, unfamiliar, even antagonistic, we can learn and explore the world and ourselves, moving toward the goal of discovering our inherent excellence.

Wendell is an African American who has done quite well in the world. He is a veteran of the civil rights movement, having picketed, marched, and been to jail for participating in sit-ins and a couple of fistfights over racist jokes. He now has a small but successful management consulting firm.

One late Friday afternoon he was dropping a report off at a client's office. The client's staff was having its weekly beer party and invited him to join. Having nothing pressing to do, he accepted the invitation. Several of the staff were telling jokes. One fellow in particular, Herb, seemed to relish relating a mixture of tasteless stories, some with a racist tinge to them.

Wendell, with caution born of maturity and some empowerment training, decided not to challenge Herb directly. After a few moments' consideration, he decided to be curious instead. During a lull he quietly asked Herb, "Are you a racist?" The room became very quiet. After a pause for reflection Herb responded with a single word: "Yes." To that Wendell said, "I thought so, but I wasn't sure. Will you tell me how that came about?" What ensued was a two-hour conversation involving all the party's participants. They discussed their beliefs about people who are different and how they came about those beliefs from particular incidents, their parents, teachers, friends, and the environment in general. The company used this incident to develop a multicultural diversity training program with Wendell and Herb as the trainers.

Being curious not only allows us to learn about that which is unfamiliar or different but also helps us learn about ourselves.

Suzanne is a woman in her middle thirties. She is a successful professional in the field of her choice. The only hole in her happiness is she is not married. Family and friends acknowledge that she is attractive and personable. They believe that she must not really want to be married since she has had more than her share of suitors, all of whom she has found wanting. Suzanne, however, is quite clear that her biggest desire is to marry, the ideas of her family and friends notwithstanding. Until recently she was certain that the only thing between her and marriage was meeting the right guy.

As she increasingly felt her biological clock ticking away, she began to wonder, be curious about the possibility that her lack of marriage might be due not to the shortcomings of the men she had dated but to some quirk in her own personality. She used curiosity, albeit driven by her desire for children, to find a psychotherapist who could guide her in her search through her psyche.

To be brief, she discovered that she was afraid of ever committing herself to anyone whom she could not completely trust to stay with her always. Of course, no one could meet such a criterion. The untenableness of the fear was such that she had repressed her entire childhood history of having been repeatedly passed from pillar to post by her parents as they tried to deal with their own fears of, and difficulties with, their mutual unfaithfulness.

Through her curiosity about herself, Suzanne learned about her fears, how to confront them safely, and how to make them an ally rather than an enemy in her search for a fulfilling mate. She learned how to use her fear as a trigger for refocusing her energy on discovering why she was being fearful. In this way, she could restabilize her relationships before her fear became so great that she felt compelled to leave them. The method worked so well that today, Suzanne is happily, though sometimes fearfully, married with twin baby girls.

Being curious is powerful and empowering. Yet, to be consistently curious requires us to discipline ourselves accordingly. When we feel the finite, self-protective pull of insisting on our rightness, of withdrawing, or of claiming ourselves as victims, we must use our discipline to become curious about the automatic nature of such reactions. We can then empower ourselves to see if those reactions are truly in our best interests. We can see if further curiosity about the differences we use to trigger our reactions might be much more useful and empowering.

Speaking Powerfully

Another very powerful way of supporting our inherent excellence is speaking powerfully through improving the efficiency and impact of our verbal communications. The raison d'etre for such power comes from the following dynamic: We speak as we think, we think as we feel, and we act as we think and feel. Thus, we can change how powerfully we act by changing how powerfully we speak. Many of us dismiss the issue of powerful speaking as "quibbling with semantics." However, we *can* change our patterns of behavior by changing our patterns of speaking. Such is the power of our inherent excellence!

The components of speaking powerfully that we will examine are speaking intentionally, speaking responsibly, speaking without self-diminishment, and speaking straight.

Speaking Intentionally. To speak powerfully, we must first clearly know what we want to say and why we want to say it. Much too often we begin speaking automatically, without having a clear, specific idea of the results we intend to achieve from our speaking. Consequently, we often confuse those who are listening to us or give them an impression we did not intend to convey. Speaking is an act of communication through which we hope to elicit a particular response or kind of response from our audience. We *never* speak purposelessly or without intention! People say "Oh, I was just thinking out loud. I didn't mean anything by that" after having made some comment that was taken the wrong way. Yet, even thinking out loud has an intention—that of clarifying our thinking. In such a case, of course, we would do best to speak quietly or let our audience know that we are just thinking out loud.

Usually it is unnecessary to clarify absolutely (specify in full detail) our intentions, because the consequences of not doing so are minimal or easily rectified, as in casual conversation. There are other times, however, when what we have to say can make a difference in a situation, and thus clarity is of utmost importance to us. Circumstances in which significant relationships, tasks, or deadlines are at stake require clear and unequivocal speaking. By taking time before speaking to clarify for ourselves our intention in speaking, we allow ourselves the opportunity to choose precisely the words and the emotions that will best convey our desired meaning.

Clarifying our intention before speaking also gives us the opportunity to consider fully whether our listener is ready to hear what we have to say; if our listener is not ready, we can then attempt to stimulate that readiness. Most of us have been in situations in which our frustration with an inattentive audience has led us to raise our voices, which tends to accomplish little more than make us hoarse. Instead, we might attempt another approach.

Clark, the sales manager of a small manufacturing firm, was poring over his sales charts when his secretary, Diane, stormed into his office insisting that she was going to fire Claire, one of the file clerks in the office. Her presentation to Clark was, to say the least, vociferous and impassioned. Clark was horrified at the thought of losing Claire. Her 25 years of highly dependable service with the firm made her in large part the backbone of his office. His immediate response was to ask Diane to reconsider her decision. Still upset, she burst into tears, saying, "If she stays, I go!" Now Clark was in a real quandary because Diane was just as valuable to him as Claire. In his intention to save Claire, he had put himself at risk with Diane.

At this juncture Clark sat back to take stock of this situation. He clarified his goal: to somehow keep both employees. To do that, he figured he had to get Diane to calm down so that she could focus attention on him and listen. In trying to come up with an idea about how to do that, he remembered a communications exercise from a program that he had taken several years ago with Don Klein and Michael Broom. More specifically, he remembered one of them saying, "If you want someone to listen to you, it works to listen to them first." With that in mind, he refocused his attention on the still-sobbing Diane and said, "OK, let's both slow down. Tell me again what happened."

This time Clark encouraged Diane to tell her full story without interruption. As he listened he made sounds of interest, sympathy, and encour-

agement, but not necessarily of agreement. After she had finished speaking he noticed that she was much calmer, looking at him as if to say, "What do we do now?" She was ready to have a reasonable conversation with him. By listening fully until Diane was completely done, he had created an audience who was ready to listen to him present his views on the situation and to work toward a resolution that would benefit both of them.

In other words, through speaking powerfully *and* listening powerfully, we give our communicating a greater probability of attaining the full impact of our clear and specific intentions.

Speaking Responsibly. The following is based John and Joyce Weir's work on percept language (1989), a powerful way of speaking responsibly. Using percept language, we base what we say on the understanding that we are responsible for our thoughts, feelings, and actions. In contrast, we normally speak in concept or object language, which assumes that we have little or no control over our thoughts, feelings, and actions. We are highlighting three rules as follows:

1. Move the locus of control of our thoughts, feelings, and actions from "out there" to "in here."

Concept Language	Percept Language
You made me think you loved me.	I made myself think you loved me.
You make me angry.	I anger myself.
That makes me sad.	I sadden myself.
My boss made me work late last night.	I made myself work late last night.

I control my own feelings. I control my own thoughts. And, I control my own actions. No one other than I can "do" my feelings, thoughts, and actions. Speaking perceptually, we give ourselves the opportunity to choose how we respond to our feelings. If "you make me angry" there is little I can do to control you. If "I anger me," I can choose to continue to anger myself, stop angering myself, or even laugh at myself if I wish.

2. Use active rather than passive statements.

Concept Language	Percept Language
I have no choice.	I give myself no choices.
I'm angry.	I anger myself.
I am aware that . . .	I make myself aware that . . .
A thought just occurred to me.	I think . . .

I am in charge of my anger, my confusion, my very life when I use verbs actively. Again, speaking perceptually, we give ourselves choices about *how* we are. If "I have no choice," there is little I can do about this state of being. If "I give myself no choices," I can choose to continue accordingly or give myself more choices and, most importantly, recognize that I am in charge of how I "do" myself. If "I am angry," I anger is who I am and there is little I can do about this passive state of being. If "I anger myself," I can actively choose to continue to anger myself, stop angering myself, or even laugh at myself if I wish to.

3. Move the locus of our interpretations from "out there" to "in here."

Concept Language	Percept Language
This is a gorgeous sunset.	My experience of this sunset brings to mind the gorgeous part of me. ("Sunset" is real, thus *out there*; but "gorgeous" is *my* interpretation, thus *in here*.)
You are really beautiful when you smile.	I experience you as the really beautiful part of me when you smile. ("You" is real; "really beautiful" is interpretation.)

Many of us speak of what is going on in our minds as if it were actually happening in external reality. It isn't! We speak as if our interpretations of external reality are really a part of external reality. They aren't! Much of our finite behavior, however, comes from the belief that our interpretations are a part of external reality and therefore available to everyone. Accordingly, anyone not in agreement with *our* interpretations is mistaken or simply wrong as we create one more finite, win/lose situation. Through owning our interpretations of external reality, as distinct from the external reality, we give ourselves the opportunity to be in charge of our interpretations which trigger our emotions which trigger much of our behavior as we explored in the previous chapter. We also give ourselves the chance to make ourselves aware of parts of ourselves that we may not have previously recognized.

Though the vocabulary of percept language is no different than normal, its syntax feels awkward and cumbersome. Speaking so can feel awkward, if not embarrassing. We imagine that people listening to us are thinking, "That person's really lost it now." Upon checking, the reactions are more of interest and include an appreciation of our openness and lack of offensiveness. Even if you do not openly speak in percept language, be sure to speak internally in percept language if empowering yourself is important to you.

Speaking without self-diminishment. We empower ourselves as we cease to "trash" ourselves. In their Self-Differentiation Workshops, the Weirs use the term *trash* for the ways we speak that diminish us or what we are saying. "I probably don't know what I'm talking about, but . . ." is trash. "I don't mean to interrupt, but . . ." is trash. "I'm sorry, but . . ." is trash. "I hate to tell you this, but . . ." is trash. "I guess . . ." when we are really certain, is trash. Qualifying words such as *probably, maybe,* and *perhaps* are often trash. For example, "*Maybe,* if you could *possibly* find the time, could you *perhaps* fix the sink today?" invites the sink-fixer to fix your sink later rather than sooner. The statement "Please fix the sink today" does not diminish the request and is more likely to produce the desired result.

Many of us trash ourselves by apologizing much too readily for any negative event whether or not we have had anything to do with that event. Have you ever apologized when someone stepped on *your* toe or bumped into *you*? We often apologize when someone is angry or hurt, as if we were in charge of their feelings. Just as others cannot cause our thoughts, feelings, or actions, we cannot cause those of others and need not disempower ourselves with guilt as we often do.

We seem to have much greater difficulty living according to the idea that we are not responsible for the feelings, thoughts, and actions of others than we do living according to the idea that others are not responsible for our feelings, thoughts, and actions. Why this is so is not clear, but if we work at changing our perceptions despite the difficulty, we will experience greater power and freedom as well as much less guilt. We are not suggesting that we do not have responsibility for how we use the influence that others have granted us; we are saying that we are *not* responsible for the feelings, thoughts, and actions that others might choose, consciously or unconsciously, to expend energy on.

Speaking straight. Most of us believe that we speak clearly and directly. If you think about it and begin to listen carefully, you will notice that we often do not. Our socialization has taught us to speak circumspectly to avoid conflict, hurting others' feelings, or rejection. We ask questions: "Don't you think you should stop spending so much money?" We make weak statements: "I think you should stop spending so much money." We offer hints: "Our money is getting low." We make facetious jokes: "You're going to put us in the poorhouse." Often we speak so softly and with so little emotion that no one hears us or understands how much we really care. These are just a few examples of ineffectual ways of speaking that we too often use and that commonly leave us wondering why what we say is so easily ignored. Sometimes we give up and say nothing at all.

To speak powerfully, speak straight. The power of the following increase with each example.

1. Request the action you want: "Will you, please, spend less money?"

2. Demand the action you want: "Stop spending so much money."

3. Be specific about the action you are demanding: "Only spend money on things that we have budgeted."

4. Speak passionately. Use your emotional energy to let others know how strongly you feel about what you want them to do.

5. Be persistent. Don't give up. Negotiate for what you want until you and the other person are fully satisfied. If you do choose to give up, know that you are making that choice. Don't blame the other person for your giving up.

6. Be clear about what you will do if you get what you want and what you'll do if you don't get it: "I'll agree to budgeting for the new stereo system you want if you stay within our budget. I'm going to open my own checking account if you don't."

Speaking straight supports the clarity and openness that the infinite game requires. Whereas straight talk does not guarantee that we will get what we want, it does increase its probability. Playing the infinite game, we are clear that our fears of conflict, hurting others' feelings, and rejection are from old tapes and stories. We are clear that they are offering us rules that we can now play *with* rather than within.

So speak with clear intention. Speak as if you are responsible for your feelings and interpretations. Speak without diminishing yourself or what you are saying. Speak straight. Try it! You'll make a difference in your life and the lives of those to whom you are speaking.

Developing A Support System

To stay focused on, to be passionate about, and to act on our inherent excellence and our preferred future; to own our shadows; to be responsible for our thoughts, feelings, and actions; to speak straight and responsibly without self-diminishment; to play 100 percent—to do all of these things is extraordinary. Our lifelong training has been in the win/lose perspective of the finite. Our tapes of self-doubt are incredibly persistent, and most of our friends and colleagues have their own versions of them. We cannot consistently trust ourselves to stay with the infinite perspective, to be aware of our own inherent excellence, and to stay focused on our preferred future. To be extraordinary and true to our inherent excellence, we need help.

We need help from like-minded people who have committed themselves to their own empowerment. We need them to remind us of our commitment to our preferred future, of our inherent excellence, of the possibilities of the infinite perspective. We need them to remind us that we are extraordinary when we give ourselves "mind attacks" of self-doubt and fear, when others that we care for don't want us to change, and when we forget that who we are is infinite.

At first glance it might seem that such people are few and far between. Not so, though they might be people who seem unlikely. Good sources of support could come from any or all of the following four categories of people.

1. People you know or with whom you are acquainted who seem to be already on their journey of empowerment. People you meet in empowerment-related workshops would fit into this category.

2. Friends, family, and loved ones (especially your children).

3. Professional colleagues, including bosses and subordinates.

4. People you don't like or who seem not to like you.

Numbers one and two are fairly obvious, although we often do not see our children as possible sources of this type of support. Actually, our children are very good at this. They hesitate less than most adults to give us straight feedback (ask any parent whose children want them to stop smoking) unvarnished with the scrupulous tact learned later. Also, their commitment to us and love is undaunted enough to withstand our disapproval. Adult socialization too often weakens such strength.

Because we spend a great deal of time with them, professional colleagues, bosses, and subordinates are good candidates for our empowerment. They have as strong an impact on us as do our families and those who know us as well, albeit in a different way. Notice whether you have any finite rules that say it would be inappropriate to ask such people to support your empowerment efforts. If you have such finite rules, simply take note that you have those rules and ask anyway.

People you don't like or who seem not to like you may strike you as odd, counterproductive sources of support. Translating this category into percept language, however, helps us understand how we can use our perceptions of these people to support us. The translation would be, "The part of me that I don't like or the part of me that doesn't like me." Or, more simply, "The not liking me part of me." Those people that we like the least provide us with a powerful opportunity to learn about ourselves.

From the first day they met, Vince couldn't stand Vickie. To his ears she whined much too much. She always seemed to be trying to impress someone. She just didn't seem real. Fortunately, Vince talked about Vickie with his wife, Michelle, who knew about percept language. With her help he translated his feelings about Vickie as follows: "The Vicki in me is the whiny part of me. The part of me that tries too hard to impress others. And the part of me that is the not real part of me." Vince's reaction to his translation didn't please him. He said, "But I never act like that! My dad was like that, and I swore I never would! It was humiliating!" He hesitated, then said, "Oh, I see! I've been using Vickie to trigger my father-part-of-me tapes! Wow, I guess I have some work to do to make peace with the whiny, phony father part of me. I also want to clean up any mess I've made with Vickie from treating her as if she were the father part of me." Michelle asked, "When are you going to do all that?

Like Vince, we can use the people we particularly don't like to do the kind of work that we have laid out for ourselves. We can also do this with the people to whom we are strongly attracted. People you would ordinarily avoid are important to have in your support group.

Once you have identified some candidates, the next step is to tell them what you want from them and to ask them to support you accordingly. Here are some ideas of what you might want them to do.

1. Remind you of your commitment to your preferred future, you inherent excellence, and the possibilities of the infinite perspective when you seem to have forgotten it.

2. Remind you that you are extraordinary when you are giving yourself mind attacks of self-doubt and fear.

3. Remind you that you are extraordinary when others whom you care for are unhappy with you because they don't want you to change.

4. Be committed enough to your empowerment to receive your disapproval, your anger, your fears, your tears with compassion and caring.

5. Be committed enough to your empowerment to persist in the face of your disapproval, anger, fears, or tears, and to continue confronting you with your inherent excellence.

Many of us have old tapes that we use to prevent ourselves from creating and using support groups for our empowerment. These tapes might tell us: "I can do it by myself"; "I shouldn't impose on others"; "They're too busy and wouldn't have time for me"; or, "They don't have that much interest in me." What do your tapes tell you? Write down their directives and comments. Rephrase them into percept language. Question them, regardless. Also, ask yourself what they want from you.

One temporary difficulty in the journey to empowerment is that we often change our friends along the way. Some dear friends and loved ones don't want us to change. They want us to stay the way we've been. Their reasons come from their old tapes about the best way to be a friend or loved one. These tapes often tell them that the way to show their love is to support us in staying safe from harm and undue risk. This is the tape that many parents followed as they were raising us. It is the tape that many of our spouses still follow. They genuinely see themselves as acting on our behalf as they try to remind us that we're not good enough, that we're too old, that we're just dreaming, that we've got responsibilities. They might also be afraid of losing us, as many parents are afraid of losing their children as they grow up and lead lives of their own. Our mates and friends may have similar fears as we move along the journey toward becoming who we want to be rather than who they want us to be.

If (1) we listen to them and their motivations with caring and compassion, (2) remain firm in our focus, (3) share our excitement, our visions, and our commitment to our own inherent excellence, then (4) invite them to join us for mutual empowerment, who knows what might happen? They may choose to join us. They may not. Either way we will be supporting their empowerment if we are clear that the choice is theirs to come or not and if we respect and value whatever choice they make. Yes, some marriages and other relationships end in this process, either agreeably or disagreeably, but to the infinite benefit of all.

Be sure to include as part of your support system empowering books, workshops, therapy, relaxation exercises, physical exercise, and spiritual or meditational exercises. We recommend the books and workshops listed in the appendix.

Being Patient with Ourselves—and Practicing, Practicing, Practicing

Being patient with ourselves means having to confront our major stories. "Get it right the first time," they say, or, "You jerk, how come you're still screwing this up?" They instill thoughts in us such as "I can't do it!" and

"It's not going to work." All these self-diminishing, self-doubting stories play the familiar theme, "I'm not sure I'm good enough," which directly contravenes our belief in our inherent excellence.

Another set of stories that routinely get in the way of empowerment is our mainly unconscious stories that have us attempting to obey or live up to the dictates of our parents, our bosses, or other persons whom we see as authority figures. When we were small we were truly dependent on our caretakers for the sustenance and shelter necessary for that survival. To risk their disapproval through disobedience or not living up to their expectations was to risk our survival. Subsequently, the tapes developed during those times were made in a manner that gives them a particular strength which persists well into our adult lives, beyond any *fact* of our dependency.

Several years ago Michael was giving a stress management seminar at a professional conference. Many of the group identified having an over-abundance of unavoidable and seemingly insurmountable work as a major stress factor. Sound familiar? When Michael suggested that they tell their bosses to limit the amount of work as a means of reducing the workload and accompanying stress, the group rebelled. One young woman, echoing the sentiments of the group, asked how would she pay her mortgage and feed her children (notice the survival issues) if her boss fired her for not doing all that was asked of her. Michael asked her if she was good at her work, to which she replied that she was very good as witnessed by the many promotions and raises that she had gotten. He then asked her how many jobs she had held and how she got them. She replied that she had held three jobs since finishing college and that she had gotten every job that she had applied for. Michael made his final point by asking her why she thought she couldn't find another job since she had had such success. She got the point. Under heavy stress is when we will particularly fall prey to our literally infantile stories of dependency upon our caretakers and our subsequent need to secure approval and be obedient.

Whether your stories are of the "I'm not sure I'm good enough" or the "I need so-and-so's approval" variety, treat these stories as you did your wandering attention in the focusing exercise. Notice the stories and what they are saying, then gently get back to empowering yourself again.

Many people, when they learn of their stories, want to focus on getting rid of them. They feel discouraged when a story they thought they had erased plays again. Our stories will not go away; they are not erasable! They are there on behalf of our survival. They are useful. Appreciate them! Then choose what you want to do.

There are times, however, when we automatically follow our stories in ways that we seem to disempower ourselves. That cannot be helped. Rather than beat yourself up or otherwise diminish yourself, try this. Notice when you have disempowered yourself or have made some sort of finite mess of a particular situation. Identify the old story that played, refocus on the infinite, and clean up any problems that you made for yourself or others who may have been involved. If you feel stuck, call on someone in your support group to help you move forward.

When you are feeling impatient with yourself, notice that time is an issue of win/lose importance only in the finite perspective. In that perspective, given the distinction of fast and slow, fast is clearly the winner and slow the loser. Consequently, much of our lives is based on getting things done quickly rather than more leisurely. Even activities that do not require speed, such as vacations, are too often done hurriedly. Activities that are best accomplished slowly are called *pain*staking. Snap decision making by individuals or small groups is a prized virtue in much of corporate America. We could wonder whether the American automobile industry wouldn't be stronger if a more *time-taking* decision-making process were used. Certainly, much of the waste in our lives and work has come from trying to accomplish too much too fast. Not only is poor productivity a result, so are our stress-induced physical and emotional ailments.

Refocus your attention on "time as opportunity," returning to the infinite perspective. If you empower yourself fully and consistently from the infinite perspective of your inherent excellence, you need not berate yourself or feel guilty for being wrong-headed or slow. Instead, use your inconsistencies as infinite learning opportunities to increase your knowledge, and appreciate the commitment your mind has to keeping you safe from harm.

CHAPTER ELEVEN:

SUPPORTING THE EMPOWERMENT OF OTHERS

We tend to speak of empowering someone. Thinking that way can quickly *get* in our way. Empowerment calls for people to *self*-discover their own inherent excellence by making their own choices. This relates to one of the key principles of influencing: We can only influence someone who chooses to be influenced by us. Accordingly, we can only offer another person the support and opportunity to empower themselves. Those we wish to empower may not have any desire to empower themselves; they may feel fine just as they are. Or, they may not want to empower themselves through accepting the opportunity that you are offering. In either case, we cannot empower others. We can only offer opportunities for them to do so as effectively as we can.

HELPING OTHERS EMPOWER THEMSELVES

Given someone interested in the empowerment opportunities we might have to offer, there is a key barrier to avoid and three steps to follow. We will deal with the barrier first: It is attaching or hooking our sense of self-esteem to the success of our empowerment efforts. We measure this by the other person changing as we desire in accordance with *our* expectations and desires for *their* inherent excellence. With our egos hooked, we can be sure that we will play the game of power finitely the moment that our success seems threatened. At that point, instead of playing infinitely, we will be trying not to lose. Having lost sight of our own infinite empowerment, no empowerment will occur as a result of anything we might do.

Our desire to empower someone frequently arises from our desire to increase our sense of satisfaction and equity in a particular relationship. There is something that *I* want for myself when I want to empower someone. My motivations may be strong or weak depending upon the situation. Generally, we motivate ourselves more strongly the more deeply we care about someone or the more deeply we feel dependent in some fashion upon that person for our own success and satisfaction. Such motivations are natural and necessary. Just be sure that you have not hooked your ego to the success of your efforts.

Three Steps for Providing Empowerment Opportunities

Three steps are useful in giving others an opportunity to empower themselves.

1. Be mindful of the person's inherent excellence.

2. Be a safety net that is willing to receive any and all of the person's energy with *compassion, appreciation,* and *curiosity.*

3. Be an energy source of unrelenting support by
    (a) unrelentingly offering your visions of the person's inherent excellence

    (b) unrelentingly being passionate about his or her empowerment

    (c) unrelentingly confronting the person with the choices that only he or she can make about how to live in a desirable way

The next scenario illustrates the barriers and the three steps.

Victor is a 42-year-old assistant director of human resources for a large transportation company. He has been very successful working with difficult employees and has a lot of pride in that fact. However, six months ago Nanci, a benefits analyst, was transferred at Victor's request to his supervision. When the transfer was first made, Jane, his boss, promised him a much-longed-for promotion and raise if he turned this woman around. Feeling very confident, he quickly bragged to his wife and friends that the promotion and raise were in the bag.

Nanci, a 40-year-old Asian-American woman, had earned herself a reputation for being hard to get along with and not very bright. If it weren't for the company's somewhat misguided Affirmative Action pro-

gram, she would have long since been fired. Just the type that Victor liked to "turn around."

With little support from previous supervisors, Nanci's work was mediocre at best. As a result she had been transferred to five different supervisors during her four years at the company. She had had only two raises during this period. Bitterness and a sharp tongue were the primary sources of her hard-to-get-along-with reputation.

For the first month Victor pretty much left Nanci alone. Over the next five months he tried to coach her toward improving her work and her relations with her fellow employees and, more important, improving how she related to the insurance vendors who were the key part of her job. She met his coaching attempts with a taciturn "Yes, sir," but made no improvement. Adding to his growing impatience, she met his attempts to befriend her with biting sarcasm, which hurt. She cursed at him and called him a racist more than once. He became outraged over this.

Nanci's bitter unresponsiveness, along with several outrageous shouting matches, have led Victor to become very wary around her. Several times he has muttered to himself, "She's hopeless."

We would need a more in-depth conversation with Victor to know if he really has hooked his ego to succeeding with Nanci or not. The fact that he has a lot of pride in "working with difficult employees" and that he has "longed for" that promotion, however, are possible indicators of his having involved his ego. In addition, it is probably very important to him to avoid the potential humiliation of not succeeding, as he has told his wife and friends that his promotion and raise are "in the bag." His hurt and outrage at having been called a racist are also indicators of his having hooked his ego to his idea of how Nanci should be treating him. He is likely to be doubting his own ability.

When we hook our egos to the success of our efforts on behalf of others, we tend to project our self-doubt onto the other person; hence, Victor mutters to himself, "She's hopeless." He has lost any awareness of Nanci's inherent excellence. Many studies in the world of education and the world of work have shown that people tend to live up to or down to our expectations of them. We cannot support them to empower themselves beyond our own attitudes and beliefs about that person.

POWER The Infinite Game

POWER The Infinite Game

POWER The Infinite Game

What choices does Victor have? If he had built an effective support group he could go to them with his frustration. As many in his position would do, he goes to see his boss. This is what happened.

"Boss, I'm stuck. Nanci has insulted me, rejected me, and in general, frustrated the hell out of me. I have no idea what to do next. Have you got any ideas at all?" After a few moments of thought, Jane said, "Well, Vic, you've got yourself in a tough spot. I've been there myself. It really hurts when it seems that despite all your efforts, you're constantly running into a brick wall."

Victor looked up at Jane and said, "Thanks, you're the first person I've talked to who seems to understand what this woman is putting me through. But I still don't know what I could do to turn her around. It's really hopeless." Jane's response to that was, "I'm really curious as to why you feel so strongly about this."

Victor said, "This is the first time in my life I've ever felt so incompetent and frustrated. Nothing I've done has worked!" To which Jane replied, "First you could choose to percept what you've been telling me and own what's going on with you. You have the ability and the background to work with Nanci. I know that!"

Getting somewhat defensive, Victor said, "I know I'm good. It's not me who's the problem, it's Nanci!" "Nonsense!" was Jane's reply. "You can either learn something about yourself here or continue to make yourself Nanci's victim. You lose, she loses, I lose, everybody loses that way. Go home tonight and reread Broom and Klein's chapters on empowerment and disempowerment. That might get you back on the right track. What do you think?"

"Well, that stuff has worked before. I'll let you know in the morning if I come up with anything," was Victor's reply. Before he left, however, he reminded Jane that his name is Victor, not Vic.

The next morning Victor met with Jane again, reporting, "Boss, Nanci's not the one who's hopeless. I'm the one who's hopeless, or rather I'm the one who's been making myself hopeless! I've got another coaching meeting with Nanci this afternoon. I'll let you know how it turns out with me in an infinite space this time." "Great," she responded. "And, I'll get off your case when you begin acting like the powerful human being I know you to be!" she added with a great deal of passion. Just as passionately she said, "I'm also very clear that what you do with Nanci is solely your choice. You've got enough credit built up with me to last you for a lifetime. So whether you choose to back off from Nanci, let her go, or turn yourself on to empowering her the way I know you can, I am behind you 100 percent. Just let me know what your choice is by tomorrow morning!" More quietly she said, *"And my name is Jane, not boss."*

Be Mindful of the Person's Inherent Excellence

This may be the most difficult of the three steps, although at first glance it seems the easiest. To ask ourselves to become aware and stay aware of another person's inherent excellence is sometimes tantamount to asking ourselves for an act of creation, a leap of faith. We require this of ourselves when we have used our stories and projections to judge someone as somehow deficient, that is, not inherently excellent. Once we make ourselves aware of these stories and their results, we have the opportunity to create for ourselves the other person's inherent excellence.

The leap of faith and act of creation are easier if our stories and projections about the other person are already positive. Jane already had an empowering story about Victor; she reminded him about it several times. *"You have the ability and the background to work with Nanci. I know that!" "And, I'll get off your case when you begin acting like the powerful human being I know you to be!" "You've got enough credit built up with me to last you for a lifetime."* All of these statements offer Victor an opportunity to remember his own inherent excellence.

The leap of faith, however, can be very difficult in the face of negative stories and projections. We can help ourselves, nevertheless, if we choose for ourselves stories of the inherent excellence of humankind. Victor and many of us have stories of this kind. We can use them to support our goal of giving others the opportunity to rediscover their inherent excellence (throughout our combined 60-plus years doing this work, we, the authors, have not talked with a single individual who could not recollect experiences of his or her inherent excellence). The problem is, we easily distract ourselves from the inherent excellence of humankind with the fears and hurts garnered by our having learned too deeply and played too well the finite game of power. When we do, we deny and hide our excellence both from ourselves and from others. Fundamentally, we must *choose* to be aware of this quality of inherent excellence in people.

Defining Inherent Excellence: An Exercise

What determines where you draw the line between those whom you consider inherently excellent and those whom you do not consider so? In your view, what actions and characteristics distinguish one group from the other? Get a sheet of paper and a pencil. Make yourself a list of those actions and the characteristics. Who comes to mind as you make your list or think about it?

While doing this exercise or thinking about doing this exercise, you may notice some reluctance or guilt creeping around your edges. Don't worry yourself. The you in me is still OK. Everyone in our society has lists of criteria they use to assign the labels of "OK" and "not OK" to people. We have a list we use at work, another with friends, another for our romances, another for children, and so on. This is everyone's pervasive and inescapable training. Since everyone has these lists and acts upon them, clearly you need infer nothing personal—even when you fall prey to them and tell yourself you should know better. You can, however, take note of these stories and then *choose*. Choose to recreate, to make the leap of faith toward making yourself aware of the inherent excellence in everyone. Include those people with whom you are struggling and about whom you are worrying. In you is the experience not only of your inherent excellence but that of everyone else as well.

Be a Safety Net That Is Willing to Receive Any and All of Another Person's Energy With Compassion, Appreciation, and Curiosity

When Victor shared his dilemma with his boss, she initially responded, "Well, Vic, you've got yourself in a tough spot. I've been there myself. It really hurts when it seems that despite all your efforts, you're constantly running into a brick wall." Victor's reply was, "Thanks, you're the first person I've talked to who seems to understand. . . ." Jane's response was, "I'm really curious as to why you feel so strongly about this."

When we have chosen the finite perspective, we deeply desire a safety net, a safe haven in which someone will respond to us with compassion, appreciation, and curiosity. When we feel safe, we relax and so can open ourselves up to new ideas and insights. When we do not feel safe, our stories tell us that any relaxation of our vigilance against losing could all too easily lead to our defeat.

Moreover, we will rarely undertake actions that seem *definitely* dangerous to the survival of our physical well-being or our sense of self-esteem or self-importance. Since our physical well-being is jeopardized only rarely in this day, age, and society, survival of our self-importance is most often what is at issue for us. If we are to offer others opportunities to empower themselves, what can we do to create this sense of safety?

Carl Rogers's phrase "unconditional positive regard" points us in the right direction. To give someone an opportunity to feel safe with us, we must be willing to be with that person without placing any conditions on how he or she should be. We are willing to be with that person along with any fear, hurt, guilt, shame, humiliation, self-diminishment, anger, or arrogance which accompanies that person. If they bring stories of their behavior of which we heartily disapprove, we will notice that such disapproval comes from *our* stories and has nothing to do with *their* inherent excellence. In acting as a safety net for someone, we express our acceptance of whatever that person may bring to us rather than express our finite, OK/not OK judgments. Thus, we present no threat, bringing instead the empowering safety of our compassion, appreciation, and curiosity.

Being a safety net for someone also requires being honest and open with the other person. If others are going to use the opportunity we offer to empower themselves, they must trust that we will be honest and straightforward. In attempting to offer a safe environment for those who come to us, we tend to commiserate and sometimes dissemble, that is, conceal our thoughts. We often attempt to be supportive by agreeing that they are in a tough spot. That's OK. However, in commiserating, we are also agreeing with their view of themselves as victims and that they can do nothing much about their situation. Imagine if Jane had said to Victor, *"I know how you must feel Victor. That Nanci is truly impossible; she should never have been hired in the first place!"*

Such "ain't it awful" commiseration does offer a safe haven. Unfortunately, it also keeps the person from empowerings owning his or her responsibilities. Although many of us commiserate or dissemble because we want to avoid the hurt or anger that our stories tell us may result if we talk straight with someone, we must remember that no opportunity for empowerment will result from such self-protective motivations.

Many of us, in the name of being open and honest, share our negative judgments and evaluations without owning them as our own. Consider Victor's appeal to Jane: *"Boss, I'm stuck. Nanci has insulted me, rejected me, and in general frustrated the hell out of me. I have no idea what to do next. Have you got any ideas at all?"* Imagine Jane, in the name of being honest and open, responding with, *"Victor you're being stupid again! Blame yourself, not Nanci! You asked for her; now you're stuck with her. Stop complaining and get on with it!"* If, in being open and honest, the person we are attempting to help discovers that we judge or evaluate them as poorly as they do, they may tend to use our evaluations to validate theirs.

To provide others with the opportunity to empower themselves, we must have compassion for their plight, an appreciation of their fundamental worthiness, and curiosity about what is going on with them. These elements infuse our honesty and shape it into a supportive tool. Consequently, we can offer this tool to others and be fairly assured that they will not mistake our concern for an attack on their already lowered self-esteem. Jane exhibited a high degree of such supportive honesty when she recognized Victor had gotten himself in "a tough spot" and went on to say, *"I've been there myself. It really hurts when it seems that despite all your efforts, you're constantly running into a brick wall. . . ."* *"I'm really curious why you feel so strongly about this."*

While exploring the potency of openness and appreciation, we may make an amazing discovery. As we allow ourselves to be *fully* open, compassionate, appreciative, and curious (hence, seemingly vulnerable), we can discover a clear, explicit, and profound sense of safety within ourselves and the world. This sense of safety within ourselves and the world communicates itself to the person to whom we wish to offer empowerment. They then feel safe enough to explore themselves and work toward their own empowerment.

Be an Energy Source of Unrelenting Support

Victor was not using his energy very effectively to facilitate Nanci's empowerment. He was expending too much of it on holding in all his frustration, worrying about his potential failure, and blaming Nanci. Jane, on the other hand, was using her energy well. From her, we can learn some ways of

(a) *Unrelentingly* offering our visions of the inherent excellence of others
(b) *Unrelentingly* being *passionate* about the empowerment of others
(c) *Unrelentingly* confronting others with the choices that only they can make about how they want to live their lives

In the first conversation, Jane told Victor, *"You have the ability and the background to work with Nanci. I know that!"* By using this and similar statements, Jane was offering to Victor her visions of his own inherent excellence. She was willing to be as persistent and unrelenting as necessary with statements reminding Victor of *his* visions of his excellence so that he could act accordingly. Given the quantity of self-diminishing stories that so many of us have, being unrelentingly reminded over and over again of our inherent excellence is a very important and often necessary gift.

The degree of passion that others exhibit when they try to help us empower ourselves becomes for us an indication of the degree to which they truly care about our empowerment. Jane unrelentingly used a great deal of passion throughout her conversations with Victor, conveying that intensity through a variety of emphatic statements; for example, *"I'll get off your case when you begin acting like the powerful human being I know you to be!"* Intensity such as this gets our attention. It also impresses us because, as we live in a society that denigrates emotions, openly expressing one's feelings can be particularly risky. Moreover, knowing that someone cares about us enough to be so passionate (and take that risk) increases the strength of our conviction that he or she really does care. We are again reminded of our inherent excellence, only this time on an emotional level; this corresponds to the intellectual reminder we receive through the actual content of what we have been told.

Finally, Jane unrelentingly confronted him with his choices and his ability to make those choices: *"First you could choose to percept what you've been telling me and own what's going on with you"*; *"You can either learn something about yourself here or continue to make yourself*

Nanci's victim"; "I'm also very clear that what you do with Nanci is solely your choice. You've got enough credit built up in my bank to last you for a lifetime. So whether you choose to back off from Nanci, let her go, or turn yourself on to empowering her the way I know you can, I am behind you 100 percent. Just let me know what your choice is by tomorrow morning!" In the process of persistently confronting him with his ability to choose, she also reaffirms that she trusts in his ability to make choices and believes in him regardless of the choices he makes.

Many of us find this extremely difficult. Little opportunity for empowerment would have been offered if Jane had said to Victor, *"Why don't you just tell her to cut out the nonsense or you'll fire her?"* or, *"I think you should just ignore her nastiness and concentrate on improving her work."* When someone brings us a problem, many of us respond automatically by telling that person what he or she *should* do rather than offering the empowerment of choice.

As we saw in earlier chapters, this is a very pervasive, deeply ingrained response to the problems and questions of others. We learned this response when we were children and our parents, teachers, and other adults told us what to do when we were likely to harm ourselves with our own choices. By too often using the advice we are offered, we remain dependent upon the thinking of others. We miss, then, opportunities to empower our ability to consciously make our own choices.

Well-intentioned friends, bosses, and parents tell us what we should do as if we still might make choices that they see as too dangerous, and thus continually reinforce these lessons. We sense this unintentional denigration and resent it. Accordingly, we often respond to "should"-oriented advice with statements like, "Yes, but I already tried that," or, "Yes, but that would take too much time." These "Yes, but . . ." statements rarely are intended to reject the actual content of the advice, but are more often focused on our desire to avoid the disparaging sense of being "treated like a child." What we want, instead, is someone to appreciate us, to listen to us, to challenge us, and to support us while we figure out our own problems. This is the essence of offering someone an opportunity to self-discover his or her own inherent excellence.

We have repeatedly emphasized the word *unrelenting.* Given all the years that we have practiced and used our stories of finite self-doubt and blame, support toward our self-empowerment must be unrelenting or we slip back into our old habits. Anything less—such as support that comes and goes, that is sometimes available and sometimes not, that waffles into commiseration at times, that allows self-diminishment to go unconfronted, that does not consistently remind us of inherent excellence, that isn't insistent about making choices—is insufficient. Too much of our society supports the safe and comfortable mediocrity that is so much a part of our lives. To truly engage in giving others an opportunity to empower themselves, we must be unrelenting. To be unrelenting is to be committed, to not give up.

Commitment is a decision regarding what we will do. Often we say we've made a commitment, then find ourselves behaving other than according to our promise. Of course, we have all sorts of very good reasons for not keeping the commitment. Such reasons might include: "I couldn't help it"; "I didn't feel like it"; "I didn't want to"; "I forgot"; "I changed my mind"; "I couldn't do it." This is not commitment. In a commitment I have given my word to myself and will not break it. Having given my word is more important than any reasons or feelings to the contrary. I will do what I said I would do because and, if necessary, only because I said I would.

In the case of empowerment, we can commit ourselves to do whatever will empower us, notwithstanding whatever fears, desires, or mitigating circumstances may arrive. This is not to imply any need for perfection in keeping commitments. Many attempts to empower are unsuccessful. No problem. At times we won't follow through on a commitment for whatever reason. At those times we have given ourselves the opportunity to reestablish our commitment and get back on track with it. The commitment might be reestablished any number of times *until we achieve the desired result.* Or, with a clear sense of responsibility we may choose to give up (rather than blame the other person or circumstances for our choice) and notify the parties affected by that choice. Such is the nature of commitment; what's important is not how many times we fail but that we continue trying until the desired result is achieved.

Jane said to Victor, *"Own what's going on with you."* Victor tried to defend himself by blaming Nanci again: *"I know I'm good. It's not me who's the problem, it's Nanci!"* Many people back off at this point because they are afraid to offend or fear the possibility of anger. Instead,

Jane retorted with her usual passion, *"Nonsense! You can either learn something about yourself here or continue to make yourself Nanci's victim. You lose, she loses, I lose, everybody loses that way."*

When do you back off? What story are you telling yourself when you do? What are your reasons for doing so? Whatever your reasons, remember they are no more than stories from the past, and that you have the choice of backing off next time or unrelentingly supporting others and yourself in the process of discovering inherent excellence.

How did Victor and Nanci turn out? We don't know. How would you choose to give Nanci an opportunity for self-empowerment? Better still, to whom would you like to give an opportunity to empower themselves? How do you plan to go about it? Who will you call upon if you get stuck?

We are inherently excellent whether we acknowledge it or not. We focus clearly, are passionate, and act accordingly whenever we decide to do so. We can be powerfully influential with those around us or stay victims to our own self-diminishment. When in low equity, we can move to get our equity up or work to take theirs down. We can count our wins and losses as we ready ourselves for our next finite struggle. Or we can live our lives from the knowledge that the infinite perspective holds the Greater Truth. This is a truth from which we give ourselves an enormous sense of humble personal power as we build societies that create harmony from our diversity and well-being for all from that harmony.

RECOMMENDED WORHSHOPS THAT EMPOWER

The Power Lab
Michael Broom and Edith Seashore
Michael F. Broom, Ph.D., Inc.
10628 High Beam Court
Columbia, Maryland 21044
410 730-1601

Self-Differentiation Workshop
John Weir, Joyce Weir, Alexandra Merrill, Michael Merrill
Weir Associates, Inc.
621 Woodbridge Street
San Luis Obispo, California 93401-5651
805 544-1754

Programs offered by the NTL Institute for Applied Behavioral Science
1240 N. Pitt Street
Alexandria, Virginia 22314-1403
800 777-5227

> *Centering for Individual and Professional Development*
> Sherman Kingsbury and Tobes Reisel
>
> *Holding On and Letting Go*
> Robert Hanna and Judith Noel or Carol Brantley
>
> *Human Interaction Workshops*
>
> > *Power: How to Create It, Keep It, and Use It*
> > Michael Broom and Katherine Eneguess
> >
> > *Self-Awareness and Being*
> > Robert Hanna and Judith Noel or Delyte Frost
> >
> > *Tavistock Workshop*
> > Harold Bridger and Nancy Brown

BIBLIOGRAPHY

Personal Power

Bach, Richard. *Illusions.* New York: Delcorte Press, 1977.

Bly, Robert. *The Little Book on the Human Shadow.* New York: Harper Collins Publishers, 1988.

Carse, James P. *Finite and Infinite Games.* New York: Random House, 1987.

Castaneda, Carlos. *Journey to Ixtlan.* New York: Simon & Schuster, 1972.

Castaneda, Carlos. *A Separate Reality.* New York: Simon & Schuster, 1974.

Castaneda, Carlos. *The Teachings of Don Juan.* New York: Ballantine, 1968.

Capra, Fritjof. *The Tao of Physics.* London: Flamingo, 1992.

Covey, Stephen R. *The 7 Habits of Highly Effective People.* New York: Simon & Schuster, 1989.

Kopp, Sheldon. *If You Meet the Buddha on the Road, Kill Him.* New York: Science and Behavior Books, Inc., 1972.

LeShan, Lawrence. *The Medium, the Mystic and the Physicist.* New York: Ballantine, 1982.

LeShan, Lawrence. *Alternate Realities.* Philadelphia, PA: Lippincott, 1976.

Maslow, Abraham. *The Farther Reaches of Human Nature.* New York: The Viking Press, 1971.

Maslow, Abraham. *Toward a Psychology of Being.* Princeton, NJ: Van Nostrand, 1968.

Rogers, Carl. *On Becoming a Person.* Boston: Houghton Mifflin Company, 1961.

Singer, June. *Boundaries of the Soul.* New York: Doubleday, 1973.

Weir, John. "The Percept Orientation." Unpublished manuscript, 1989.

Interpersonal and Group Power

Axelrod, Robert. *The Evolution of Cooperation*. New York: Basic Books, Inc., 1984.

Bach, George and Patricia Widen. *The Intimate Enemy: How to Fight Fair in Love and Marriage*. New York: Avon, 1976.

Bach, George. *Paring*. New York: Avon, 1971.

Berne, Eric. *Games People Play*. Memphis, TN: Castel Books, 1964.

Berne, Eric. *I'm OK, You're OK*. New York: Harper Collins, 1990.

Campbell, Susan M. *Beyond The Power Struggle*. San Luis Obispo, CA: Impact Publishers, 1984.

Craig, James H. and Marguerite Craig. *Synergic Power: Beyond Domination and Permissiveness*. Greenbrae, CA: ProActive Press, 1979.

Rogers, Carl. *On Encounter Groups*. New York: Harper & Row, 1970.

Schutz, William. *Joy: Expanding Human Awareness*. New York: Irvington, 1967.

Watzlawick, Paul, John H. Weakland, Richard Fisch. *Change*. New York: W. W. Norton & Company Inc., 1974.

Organizational Power

Argyris, Chris. *Interpersonal Competence and Organizational Effectiveness*. Homewood, IL: Dorsey Press, 1962.

Bacharach, Samuel B. and Edward Lawler. *Power and Politics in Organizations*. San Francisco: Jossey–Bass, 1980.

Blanchard, Kenneth H. and Spencer Johnson. *The One Minute Manager*. New York: Morrow, 1982.

Block, Peter. *The Empowered Manager*. San Francisco: Jossey-Bass, 1987.

Bothwell, Lin. *The Art of Leadership*. Englewood Cliffs, NJ: Prentice-Hall, Inc., 1983.

Hagberg, Janet. *Real Power*. Sheffield, WI: Sheffield, 1994.

Heider, John. *The Tao of Leadership*. Atlanta, GA: Humanics Limited, 1985.

Kanter, Rosabeth Moss. *The Change Masters*. New York: Simon and Schuster, 1983.

McClelland, David. *Power: The Inner Experience*. New York: Irvington Pub., 1975.

McCormick, Charles. *The Power of the People*. New York: Penguin Books, 1973.

Oshry, Barry. *Middle Power*. Boston: Power & Systems, 1980.

Senge, Peter. *The Fifth Discipline*. New York: Doubleday, 1990.

Siu, R.G.H. *The Master Manager.* Melbourne, FL: Krieger, 1980.

Siu, R.G.H. *The Way to Executive Serenity.* New York: William Morrow and Company Inc., 1980.

Suresh Srivastva and Associates. *Executive Power.* San Francisco: Jossey-Bass Inc., 1986.

Women and Power

Claremont, Irene. *Knowing Woman.* New York: Harper and Row Publishers, 1973.

Goldenberg, Naomi. *Changing of the Gods.* Boston, MA: Beacon Press, 1979.

Hall, Nor. *The Moon and the Virgin.* New York: Harper & Row, Publishers, 1980.

Harding, M. Esther. *Woman's Mysteries.* New York: Harper & Row, Publishers, 1976.

Henley, Nancy. *Body Politics.* Englewood Cliffs, NJ: Prentice-Hall, Inc., 1977.

Josefowitz, Natasha. *In a Nutshell.* San Diego, CA: Prestwick Publishing, 1982.

Loden, Marylyn. *Feminine Leadership or How to Succeed in Business Without Being One of the Boys.* New York: Times Books, 1985.

Men and Power

Bly, Robert. *Iron John.* New York: Addison-Wesley Publishing Company Inc., 1990.

Goldberg, Herb. *The Inner Male.* New York: New American Library, 1987.

Keen, Sam. *Fire in the Belly.* New York: Bantam Books, 1991.

Diversity and Power

Cross, Elsie, Judith Katz, Frederick Miller, and Edith Seashore, eds. *The Promise of Diversity.* Burr Ridge: Erwin Professional Publishing, 1994.

Davis, George and Gregg Watson. *Black Life in Corporate America.* Garden City: Anchor Press/Doubleday, 1982.

Giddings, Paula. *When and Where I Enter.* New York: Bantam Books, 1984.

Grier, William H. and Price M. Cobbs. *Black Rage.* New York: Basic Books, 1992.

Griggs, Lewis and Lente-Louise Louw. *Valuing Diversity.* New York: McGraw-Hill, 1995.

Heinton, Calvin. *Sex and Racism in America.* New York: Grove Press, Inc., 1965.

King, Martin Luther, Jr. *Stride Toward Freedom.* New York: Ballantine Books, 1960.

Kochman, Thomas. *Black and White Styles in Conflict.* Chicago: University of Chicago Press, 1981.

Morrison, Toni. *Race-ing Justive, En-gendering Power.* New York: Pantheon Books, 1992.

Pasteur, Alfred B. and Ivory L. Toldson, I. *Roots of Soul.* Garden City, NY: Anchor Press, 1982.

Schlesinger, Arthur. *The Disuniting of America.* New York: W.W. Norton & Company, Inc., 1992.

Steele, Shelby. *The Content of Our Character.* New York: St. Martin's Press, 1990.

Thomas, Roosevelt, Jr. *Beyond Race and Gender.* New York: AMACOM, 1991.

Wallace, Michele. *Black Macho and the Myth of the Super-Woman.* New York: Warner Books, Inc., 1980.

Malcolm X and Alex Haley. *The Autobiography of Malcolm X.* New York: Grove Press, Inc., 1966.

West, Cornel. *Race Matters.* Boston: Beacon Press, 1993.

Community and Social Power

Alinsky, Saul. *Reveille for Radicals.* New York: Random House, 1989.

Alinsky, Saul. *Rules for Radicals.* New York: Random House, 1989.

Chase, Stuart. *Roads to Agreement.* Los Angeles, CA: Harper, 1951.

Coser, Lewis A. *The Functions of Social Conflict.* New York: Free Press, 1964.

Foa, Uriel and Edna Foa. *Societal Structures of the Mind.* New York: Thomas, 1974.

French, John and Bertram Raven. Studies in Social Power. In *Group Dynamics, Research and Theory,* edited by Dorwin Cartwright. New York: Harper and Row, 1959.

Galbraith, John Kenneth. *The Anatomy of Power.* Boston: Houghton Mifflin Company, 1983.

Hawley, Willis D. and Frederick M. Wirt. *The Search for Community.* Englewood Cliffs, NJ: Prentice-Hall, 1974.

Hunter, Floyd. *Community Power Structure: A Study of Decision.* Chapel Hill, NC: University of North Carolina Press, 1953.

Ignatiev, Noel. "Treason to Whiteness." *Utne Reader,* No. 66 (1994), pp. 82–86.

Klein, Donald. *Community Dynamics and Mental Health.* New York: Wiley, 1968.

Liebert, Roland J. and Allen Imershein, eds. *Power, Paradigms and Community Research.* San Francisco, CA: Sage Publications, 1977.

Martin, Roscoe C., et al. *Decisions in Syracuse.* West Port, CT: Greenwood Press, 1968.

Presthus, Robert. *Men at the Top: A Study in Community Power.* New York: Oxford University Press, 1964.

Russell, Bertram. *Power.* New York: Unwin Books, 1962.

Toffler, Alvin. *Power Shift.* New York: Bantam Books, 1990.

Mythological and Spiritual Power

Campbell, Joseph. *Hero With a Thousand Faces.* Princeton, NJ: Princeton University Press, 1949.

Eliade, Mircea. *Sacred and Profane.* Orlando, FL: Harcourt Brace Jovanovich, 1959.

Harner, Michael. *Way of the Shaman.* New York: Harper & Row, Publishers, Inc., 1980.

Herrigel, Eugen. *Zen in the Art of Archery.* New York: Random House, 1953.

Lao Tsu. *Tao Te Ching.* trans. Gia-Fu Feng and Jane English. New York: Vintage Books, 1972.

Larsen, Stephen. *Shaman's Doorway.* New York: Harper & Row, 1977.

Maslow, Abraham. *Religions, Values and Peak Experiences.* New York: Viking Penguin, 1976.

Peck, Scott. *The Road Less Travelled.* New York: Simon and Schuster, 1979.

Suzuki, Shunryu. *Zen Mind, Beginner's Mind.* New York: John Weatherhill, Inc., 1970.

Wilhelm, Richard, trans. *The I Ching.* Princeton, NJ: Princeton University Press, 1967.

Other

Clayre, Alasdair. *The Heart of the Dragon.* Boston: Houghton Mifflin, 1985.

Goodman, Dennis. "Schools that Fail the Students," *The Washington Post,* 3 November 1991, sec. C, p. 3.

Langer, Susanne. *Philosophy in a New Key.* Cambridge, MA: Harvard University Press, 1957.

Skinner, B. F. *Beyond Freedom and Dignity.* New York: Knopf, 1971.